In the
Shadow of
the Great
White Way

To Garry Watson!

Peace & love 2950

Bul S

Enjoy!,

Paul Carter Harrison

2/1996

IN THE SHADOW OF THE GREAT WHITE WAY

Images from the Black Theatre

Photographs by Bert Andrews
Text by Paul Carter Harrison and Bert Andrews
Introduction by Cicely Tyson

THUNDER'S
MOUTH
PRESS

Photographs © 1957-1989 by Bert Andrews
Text © 1989 by Paul Carter Harrison and Bert Andrews
Introduction © 1989 by Cicely Tyson

Published by Thunder's Mouth Press, 54 Greene Street, Suite 4S, New York, NY 10013.

First edition.
First printing, 1989.

Library of Congress Cataloging in Publication Data:

Andrews, Bert.
    In the shadow of the great white way ; images from the Black
    theatre / photographs by Bert Andrews ; text by Paul Carter Harrison
    and Bert Andrews : introduction by Cicely Tyson.
       p.   cm.
    ISBN 0-938410-81-4 : $38.50
    ISBN 0-938410-98-9
    1. Afro-American theater—New York (N.Y.)—Pictorial works.
I. Harrison, Paul Carter, 1936-   . II. Title.
PN2270.A35A53   1989
779'.9792'0899607307471—dc20

89-20302
CIP

Excerpt from "Note on Commercial Theatre" by Langston Hughes © 1948 by Alfred A. Knopf, Inc. Reprinted
from *Selected Poems of Langston Hughes,* by permission of Alfred A. Knopf, Inc.

Designed by Hannah Lerner.

Manufactured in the United States of America.

Distributed by Consortium Book Sales, 213 East 4th Street, St. Paul, MN 55101 (612) 221-9035.

For the memory of
my mother and brother
Frieda Louise Andrews
and
Emmett "Lucky" Andrews

You've taken my blues and gone—
You sing 'em on Broadway
And you sing 'em in Hollywood Bowl,
And you mixed 'em up with symphonies
And you fixed 'em
So they don't sound like me.
Yep, you done taken my blues and gone. . . .

But someday somebody'll
Stand up and talk about me,
And write about me—
Black and beautiful—
And sing about me,
And put on plays about me!
I reckon it'll be
Me myself!

Yes, it'll be me.

Langston Hughes
From *"Note on Commercial Theatre"*

Contents

Pictorial Chronicle of Black Theater Lost

"The entire history of the black theater has been lost."

Those were the words of Deborah Ryan of the Schomburg Center for Research in Black Culture when she learned yesterday that a fire had destroyed nearly all of the photographic works of Bert Andrews.

Her description was not much of an exaggeration. Mr. Andrews, a commercial photographer, has chronicled 30 years of black theater productions on and off Broadway.

"I have the complete Negro Ensemble Company from the start to now," Mr. Andrews said, "the New Federal Theatre, more than a thousand shows, more than 100,000 negatives."

"When I say I'm wiped out," he said, "you got to understand I don't even know who owes me money."

Until Tuesday, Mr. Andrews had his studios on the fourth floor of 750 Eighth Avenue, at West 46th Street. At 11:26 P.M., the first of four fire alarms was sounded there. The blaze was not under control until 3 o'clock the next morning. . . .

The New York Times
February 2, 1985

Photo Studio Fire Not All Negative

For Bert Andrews, photographer, it has been like digging up—reconstructing—an entire civilization. His own.

On Jan. 29, 1985, an all-night fire devoured his studio at 750 Eighth Avenue at the corner of 46th Street. "Totally destroyed everything. Wiped me out. I got out of it a couple of burned cameras I'm keeping as mementos. One I'm making into a whata-macallit, a paperweight."

Lost forever in the fire were "some 40,000 to 50,000 images, of which I'm hoping to recover 10,000." The lost images were of 30 years of theater productions, primarily black theater, in and out of the city—a priceless archive stretching back to "Dark of the Moon" at the Harlem YMCA in 1955 (Cicely Tyson, Roscoe Lee Brown, Clarence Williams III, directed by Vinette Carroll). . . .

He has spent the past two years in a great detective hunt—or archeological dig.

"First thing, I went back to the theater companies"—the Negro Ensemble Company, the New Federal Theatre, the Frank Silvera Workshop, the Richard Allen Cultural Center—"to see what *they* had." They had a surprising lot—almost 2,000 prints were unearthed at NEC alone. . . .

A Bert Andrews Photographic Collection of Blacks in the Theatre has been established at the Schomburg Center of the New York Public Library, 515 Lenox Avenue (135th Street). There were dedication ceremonies yesterday, along with the opening of an exhibit of 28 of the prints.

The fire, says Andrews, turned out to be a mixed blessing—"though my favorite expression now is: Deliver me from mixed blessings. But thanks to the fire, finally, 30 years later, I discovered that what had been a job was now a history."

The New York Post
September 23, 1988

Acknowledgements

I have received the invaluable support of friends, family members, and organizations during my career. After the fire that destroyed my collection in 1985, their continued support of my work helped me to produce this book. I am deeply grateful to the following:

Leon Denmark and Douglas Turner Ward of the Negro Ensemble Company, for providing work space and other forms of assistance.

Producer and director Woodie King, Jr. of the New Federal Theatre, for allowing me the benefit of his vast knowledge of Black Theatre.

Producer Linda Herring of the New Federal Theatre, for her able assistance in restoring the theatre's collection.

Howard Dodson, chief of the Schomburg Center for Research in Black Culture, for providing support and encouragement, and Deborah Willis, photographic archivist at the Schomburg, for the assistance given me in cataloguing photographs.

Press agents Max Eisen, Howard Atlee, and Ben Morse, and the Jeff Richards organization, for allowing me access to their files.

Friends Dorothy Ross, Sally Sears, Rose Smith, Ida Lewis, Norman Rothstein, Julie Rothstein, Robyn Govan, Gerald Krone, Dorothy Olim, and Lloyd Richards, for their encouragement, advice, and support.

Diane Aubrey and Terrie Williams, who formed the Friends of Bert Andrews Committee, for raising the funds necessary to help me get back on my feet after the fire.

Joan Sandler and Gloria Mitchell, for raising funds that enabled me to reconstruct my files.

Carmen de Jesus and Joseph Griffith, for their friendship and for the assistance given me in copying, developing, and printing.

Dr. Andrew Ghio, for his friendship and financial support.

Victor Salupo, a friend, for his expertise, wisdom, and special assistance.

Uncle Louis Hudson; aunts Bernice Hudson, Dolly Hudson, Louise Johnson, Lillian Merchant, and Mildred Jones; and cousins Al Johnson, Marsha Hudson, Carl Johnson, and Barbara Escobar; for their unswerving support—for always being there when I needed them.

Marie Brown, for her advice and interest.

I am fortunate to have worked with a number of talented people on this book. I am indebted to writer Paul Carter Harrison for shaping my ideas into final prose. Special thanks goes to the publisher Neil Ortenberg, and to the fine team of editors—Michael Schwartz, Peter Erdmann, Ingrid Geerken, Jean Casella, and Richard Derus—with whom I worked at Thunder's Mouth Press. And I owe a special debt to my agent Claudia Menza, who believed in this project and stayed with it all the way.

The foundations and organizations that are mentioned in this book were extremely helpful in providing financial support. I thank them for their assistance.

And above all, I thank Barrie Novak, my special friend of thirty years, for her advice, encouragement, understanding, support, and, most important, love.

Bert Andrews
July 1989

Introduction
by Cicely Tyson

FATE HAS A WAY of finding us at certain times in our lives. It found Bert and me one day, many years ago, as our paths crossed on Eighth Street in Greenwich Village.

We were both young, unknown, and determined to break through uncharted ground. Bert was a photographer for the *Amsterdam News* at the time, shooting the jazz scene, club circuit, entertainment places like Harlem's famous Apollo, "weddings, babies, and bar mitzvahs." I was a model and was studying acting. Neither Bert nor I had any idea at the time that we would ever be successful enough to earn a living in the professions we had chosen; we did know, however, that we loved the creative challenge. Though work was not easy to come by in the exclusive realms we each envisioned mastering, we never set our sights lower than our goals.

Walking down Eighth Street that afternoon, I noticed a man on the other side of the street cross over to my side, as if he knew me and intended to speak to me. He had a camera slung over his shoulder and a camera bag filled with equipment. We had not met before and I did not know his name; yet I vividly remembered his face from somewhere. He introduced himself as Bert Andrews, photographer, and said he had worked for Chuck Stewart, who photographed me for the cover of *Our World* magazine. He then asked if I could use more pictures for my portfolio, and during the conversation that followed, I found myself staring at him, struggling to place where and when I had seen his face before.

Then it came to me. Some years earlier, I had seen him at a wedding I attended with my family. I remember being mesmerized, not by the camera in his hands, but by his face. It was an arresting face. There was a gentleness and kindness there, a depth I could not define. We were not introduced and I never saw him again until this moment. Here he was, standing before me, asking if he could photograph my face!

We arranged an appointment, the first of many. We began to date, and soon after, became fascinated with one another's work. So began a lifelong friendship that not only paralleled, but even played a major role in each of our professional lives.

Looking back now on this innocent time when the world lay before us "like a land of dreams," I think of how deeply I believe that nothing is a random throw of the dice. Many people believe life is just a series of meaningless events and coincidences; but I am not one of these people. When I remember the extraordinary reaction I experienced seeing Bert Andrews that first time, I am reminded of the divine threads in the tapestry of life, the design of which we may not understand, but are struck by at certain moments in our lives that stand apart from all others.

During the time we were dating, I was chosen for my first starring role on stage in the play *Dark of the Moon*, directed by Vinnette Carroll at the Harlem YMCA. (For those young readers new to the world of theatre, Vinnette Carroll, the first black female director in theatre, brought gospel to Broadway in such award-winning productions as *Black Nativity*, *Your Arms Too Short to Box with God*, and *Don't Bother Me, I Can't Cope*.) When I learned that Vinnette was searching for a photographer, I recommended my friend Bert. They met, he was hired, and Bert Andrews has not stopped shooting theatrical productions since.

Over the years, Bert labored through many a sleepless night, struggling to get a photograph just right. A consummate artist and perfectionist, he was obsessively vigilant about capturing exactly what he saw through his lens. I remember how frustrating it was for him when he thought he was finished in the darkroom, only to study the results of his hours of developing, sigh wearily, crumple the proofs in his hand, throw them away, and march back into the darkroom to start all over again. I would pick up the discarded photographs, and wonder what was wrong with them, since they looked perfectly fine to me. But his demands for perfection, the artistic standards he set for himself, were inviolate and known to him alone. And he was always right.

Bert always looked as if he was carrying his life on his shoulders—cameras hanging from his neck, leather bags brimming over with film, strobes and other equipment tied around his waist. He was a walking photography studio. The camera was his Muse. Burdened by all the technical equipment necessary for his work, his body leaned to one side from the weight of his service. Body and soul—he was and is completely and utterly devoted to his work. It never asked too much of him.

2

Yet jobs never came easily for Bert. It was a continual struggle, despite how gifted he was and how highly he came to be regarded for the quality of his work. I was with him during those heartbreaking moments when the work he needed so badly was awarded to someone else, less talented perhaps, who knew the right people or happened to be the "right" color for the job. There were terribly lean periods. And while I always had my typing pool to fall back on between acting jobs and modeling, Bert had nothing else. If he did not shoot a picture, he had nothing.

As I retrace our friendship since those early days, I am struck by the influence he has had on my life. It was Bert's introduction of me to author Paule Marshall that resulted in my first starring television role as Serena in *Brown Girl, Brown Stones*. And I cannot deny that my passion for photography, which led to photojournalism assignments for the *New York Times* and *Ebony* magazine, was enhanced by our friendship.

Many years have passed since that day we first met on Eighth Street in the Village, and I again think of fate. Someone stops you in the street and alters the course of your life. Bert calls it a "little twist of fate," while I think of it as divine guidance. Whatever it's called, I am grateful for having met him and having shared our gift of friendship.

The publication of *In the Shadow of the Great White Way* is an especially important event. It is the very first book of its kind, the *only* visual testament bearing witness to the living black dramas that burst onto the American stage with such imaginative force that American theatre was never the same again. The vision and genius of black writers, performers and directors—together with all those black artists who shaped the culture of this century and made it so uniquely American—not only expressed the yearnings of so many captive and broken generations, forced to be history-less, family-less, job-less, country-less, liberty-less, but also helped lead the way to the heroic civil rights movement in that explosive decade that changed the course of history.

While Martin Luther King and others were making history on the front lines, we were mirroring the history being made. While many of us were so involved in the making of theatre history, Bert Andrews was able to stop time and freeze that history being made: from Jean Genet's *The Blacks*, which launched *avant garde* theatre in America, to Lorraine Hansberry's *To Be Young, Gifted, and Black*, Athol Fugard's *Bloodknot*, and Amiri Baraka's *The Toilet* and *The Slave*.

That a book of this kind has never been published before makes me realize that there is only one Bert Andrews, therefore only one such photographic record possible.

I shudder to think that all of this might have been lost forever in the catastrophic fire that reduced Bert's photographs to ashes in 1985. His entire life's work was almost destroyed in one night and this priceless history of nearly three decades of theatre arts along with it. Were it not for the hundreds of photographs that poured in from all who knew, loved, and valued Bert's accomplishments, we would never be privy to these special renderings of American dramatic art at its most pivotal time.

I am reminded of what Alex Haley wrote so poignantly in his introduction to *Roots*: "Finally, I acknowledge an immense debt to the griots of Africa, where today it is rightly said that when a griot dies, it is as if a library burned to the ground." That's how close we came to losing this "library."

In the Shadow of the Great White Way is not just a picture book. It is a treasury of a special time for all of us . . . for those who stood upon the stage, for those who viewed from the audience, and for all those who witness now for the first time the landmark era of which we speak.

Historical Notes

BROADWAY, THE GREAT WHITE WAY, has long been a spectacle of awe-inspiring incandescence for the fledgling performing artist who resides on the edge of its penumbra. To bask in the lights of Broadway has meant instant celebrity and recognition. Those who performed in the shadow of the Great White Way were presumed destined for obscurity, particularly if the product produced was not fashioned in accordance with Broadway's standard of commercial wisdom or popular taste. Yet Black Theatre, in style and content, has emerged from the shadow of the Great White Way to receive legitimacy as a unique experience in the American theatre, and an expression of the integrity of African-American culture.

The Black Theatre Movement, in its present configuration, is the direct result of the past twenty-five years of African-American social and cultural activism. However, its roots are deeply fixed in the evolvement of the American theatre as a legitimate cultural resource. The colonial American encounter with theatre consisted of English imports designed as elite entertainment for the landed gentry, who wished to separate themselves from the barroom cabarets indulged in by settlers with less social fortune. As early America began to develop its own voice with a more egalitarian theatre that embraced the common interests of American people, the presence of the African-American experience in these dramatizations was conspicuously absent or woefully distorted, despite the intimacy blacks shared with whites in the forming of the nation, both economically and culturally.

The first indigenous American play is reputed to be *The Prince of Parthia* in 1767. Soon after, in 1769, Lewis Hallam's comedy *The Padlock* introduced the first black character to the American stage in the form of a grossly comic slave named Mungo. It was not until the 1776 appearance of John Leacock's *The Fall of British Tyranny* that blacks were presented in a drama which dealt with the complexity of black and white relationships during the American Revolution. While freed slaves fought for liberty and equality, African Americans would continue to be misrepresented in the evolution of the American theatre right into the nineteenth century.

Until the early nineteenth century, black participation in the theatre was based on imitation of the forms of entertainment that were legitimized by the cultural establishment. The Park Theatre, which featured English actors, was one of the oldest theatrical institutions in New York. Among regular visitors to the segregated section of the theatre were two fledgling black actors, James Hewlett and Ira Aldridge, who were great admirers of these performances. So impressed were they that Hewlett, who became anointed as America's first black tragic actor, organized a company of black actors into the African Grove Theatre in 1820, with the sole purpose of performing Shakespearean dramas. The company performed in lower Manhattan to a mixed audience, but was rebuked by an intolerant press and rudely jeered by white hooligans. After the company collapsed, Ira Aldridge, acknowledged as the second great black tragedian, left for England in 1824, and went on to win wide fame and acclaim in Europe as a Shakespearean actor.

By 1828, a new form of theatrical entertainment was in its embryonic stages. Thomas Dartmouth Rice, a white American performer, created the gross image of a shuffling, singing slave in the character of "Jim Crow." In 1833 the act was expanded to include an impish child in burnt-cork makeup, who was dumped onto the stage from a bag. The blackfaced imp would then mock the shuffling dance steps of Rice, who also sang modified slave songs which he called "Bone Squash." The act was called the "first Ethiopian opera." Rice's "Coon show" led to the development of the full-scale minstrel shows—a chorus of cork-faced white entertainers—which received popular acclaim when Daniel Emmett brought the Virginia Minstrels to the New York stage in 1843. Ironically, it could be said that minstrelsy, which basically appropriated black life and held it up for ridicule, became the only authentic theatrical form to be created in America. Blacks, however, were not admitted into minstrelsy as performers until after the Civil War. And while the popular theatrical entertainment was the precursor to American vaudeville and provided an opportunity to train many black performers for the stage, blacks wearing cork-face—actually imitating whites imitating caricatures of blacks—merely served to advance stereotypes of black life to a wider audience.

Prior to the introduction of blacks onto the popular stage in minstrelsy, efforts had been made to dignify the humanity of the slave through abolitionist melodramas such as Harriet Beecher Stowe's *Uncle Tom's Cabin*. While Tom was indeed intended to be heroic, his character inadvertently propagated the stereotype that blacks were fundamentally docile and submissive. The play was a popular success, opening in New York in 1852 and having continued popularity among American audiences until 1931. However, for future generations of African Americans, Tom's heroic, even rebellious persona remained obscured by what was perceived as a model of passivity.

The abolitionist movement also introduced the first play known to be written by an African American—William Wells Brown's *Escape: A Leap for Freedom*. The work, laced with the blackfaced buffoonery of minstrelsy, was performed by the author as staged readings to sympathetic audiences in remote spaces, away from the lights of the legitimate stage. By the end of the nineteenth century, a collection of black theatre artists became determined to destroy the minstrel structure, and set into motion the musical stage style we now recognize as the basic pattern for the twentieth-century American musical theatre form.

The turn of the century brought the Industrial Revolution, and blacks began to migrate to the North, viewing Harlem as Mecca. In 1891, Sam T. Jack, a burlesque circuit manager, introduced to a minstrel-style show, *The Creole Show*, a chorus of sixteen young black women who sang and danced. The show opened in Boston, then moved to Sam T. Jack's Opera House in Chicago, where it ran for the entire World's Fair season. John W. Isham, an advance agent for *The Creole Show*, produced *Oriental America*, breaking away from the traditional cakewalk and burlesque comic segments and replacing them with an operatic medley which featured tenor Sidney Woodward, J. Rosamond Johnson (who later collaborated with his brother to write the song "Lift Every Voice and Sing," which is widely accepted as the "Negro National Anthem"), and Inez Clough. Meanwhile, operating out of Worth's Museum in Greenwich Village, Bob Cole wrote, directed, and produced *A Trip to Coontown*, the first American musical to have a plot, thereby breaking away from the minstrel tradition. In the cast was the gifted actor, writer, and director Jesse Shipp, who later wrote *In Dahomey*, the musical that brought Bert Williams and George Walker to the Broadway stage in 1903. The music was composed by Will Marion Cook, and the lyrics by the revered poet of the period, Paul Laurence Dunbar.

The black musical had come to the Great White Way. In 1906, Williams and Walker were brought together for another musical by Shipp and Cook—*Abyssinia*, a satire which dealt with blacks returning to their cultural roots in a fabled African land. The work was criticized by most reviewers as being too artful, and lacking in the familiar song and dance style that had been the benchmark of black musical theatre. The show was followed by the Williams and Walker Company production of *Bandanna Land*, a fast-paced satirical song and dance musical which enjoyed popular success.

In Harlem, away from the bright lights and celebrity of Broadway, the beginnings of a Black Theatre Movement were taking shape. Eddie Hunter—a young playwright whose early theatre pieces in 1909 prompted the conversion of the Lincoln and Lafayette movie houses into legitimate theatres—played a leadership role in the budding movement. A prolific writer, Hunter resisted the pressure of producing entertainment that merely satisfied the tastes of the black middle class. He was one of the first of his generation to espouse the creation of a permanent theatre in Harlem as a method of revitalizing African-American culture. Henry Cramer's *The Old Man's Boy*, which appeared at the Lincoln in 1914, is credited with paving the way for serious black drama.

A year earlier, the Lafayette Theatre had presented J. Leubrie Hill's highly successful musical *Darktown Follies*, which was followed by the 1915 production of *Darkydom*, written by the comic duo of Flournoy Miller and Aubrey Lyles (who later became celebrated, along with Noble Sissle and Eubie Blake, for the 1921 Broadway sensation *Shuffle Along*.) By 1919, the Lafayette Players came into being under the managerial guidance of Lester Walton and the artistic leadership of Anita Bush—an actress who had operated a stock company at the Lincoln Theatre, and Charles Gilpin—one of the prominent actors of the period. As the first formally organized black performance company in Harlem, the company served as a training ground for developing black theatre artists as well as a producing unit for plays that portrayed blacks in roles that showed depth of character, as opposed to the stereotypes created by a narrowly focused social bias. The formation of the Lafayette Players came at a time when Harlem was about to enter the period of cultural rebirth and revitalization commonly referred to as the Harlem Renaissance.

The Roaring Twenties brought the end of World War I, and new expectations of social justice among African Americans. They also brought the Harlem Renaissance, a period which opened the way for a re-evaluation of global black art, literature, and music, thereby leading to the confirmation of a cultural history unique to African Americans. The new consciousness prompted an audience to view a production of Eugene O'Neil's *The Emperor Jones* at the Lincoln Theatre with a jaundiced eye of disapproval upon witnessing the famous Jules Bledsoe chase his shadow through the jungle with the stereotypical countenance of an ignoble savage. It was an extravagantly exciting time which boasted many luminaries in the arts, such as Langston Hughes and Florence Mills—who, though a star of the Broadway stage in *Shuffle Along* and later *Dixie to Broadway* in 1924, found her way back to culturally scintillating Harlem in *Blackbirds*, which opened at the Alhambra Theatre in 1926. As elders would note, Harlem during this period was like Paris—a city of lights. In the meantime, W.E.B. DuBois, a prominent black scholar, appealed to black theatre artists to abandon Broadway in favor of theatre experiences that were more ethnocentric. He organized the Krigway Players in Harlem in 1926 with the objective of developing black folk dramas that dealt with the specific interests of African-American people.

One of the important vestiges of the Depression of the 1930s was the emergence of social protest in the American theatre. On the Lower East Side of New York was the old Jewish Theatre, which spawned the Group Theatre. It was a company of social activists, which set its sights on developing a new method of acting under the leadership of Lee Strasberg, while performing plays that were socially significant and responsible. While the Group Theatre was giving birth to Clifford Odets's *Waiting for Lefty*, Broadway was mounting Marc Connelly's vulgarization of black religiosity, *The Green Pastures*. Though it may have vaulted many jobless black vaudevillians and actors out of the Depression, *The Green Pastures*'s irresponsible assault on the image of African Americans effectively propagated stereotypes that would reappear with greater frequency in future popular American entertainments, including the culturally myopic folk opera. Such works possessed none of the true sense of social inquiry of Hall Johnson's musical *Run, Little Children*, which played at the Lafayette Theatre in 1933, or the trenchant realism of Langston Hughes's *Mulatto*, which appeared on Broadway in 1934, featuring Rose McClendon—who in 1935 organized the Negro People's Theatre, which offered a black version of *Waiting for Lefty* as its first production at the Rockland Palace in Harlem.

The thirties also gave birth to a national, government-sponsored program known as the Federal Theatre Project, which subsidized theatre programs around the country. The Negro Unit of the FTP was located at the Lafayette Theatre, which produced works such as Frank Wilson's *Walk Together Children*, Rudolph Fisher's *The Conjure Man Dies*, and the widely celebrated Orson Welles and John Houseman adaptation of *Macbeth*, set on an exotic West Indian island and featuring Canada Lee. While significant works were produced through the FTP, other theatre groups were being formed. Among these was the Harlem Suitcase Theatre, organized in a loft by Langston Hughes, where his play *Don't You Want to Be Free* was performed with minimal stage supports in 1938. The work featured Robert Earl Jones—the father of James Earl Jones—and played weekends in the loft for a year before the production had to be moved to the basement of the 135th Street—currently the Schomburg—Library.

Toward the end of the decade, the Rose McClendon Players was organized by a Harlem social worker, Dick Campbell, in an effort to create a theatre based in Harlem that could be the home of actors, playwrights, and directors who shared a commitment to countering the cliches of black life that proliferated on Broadway. The company was coached by Theodore Komisarjevsky of the Moscow Arts Theatre, and marked the beginning of a penchant among black theatre groups for ensemble performing. Among its members were Ossie Davis, Ruby Dee, Jane White, and Frederick O'Neal (who was later elected president of Actors Equity in 1964). One of its most successful productions was William Ashley's *Booker T. Washington*, which featured Dooley—"Play it again, Sam"—Wilson and enjoyed a long Harlem run before being performed at the 1939 World's Fair.

In the early 1940s, Black Theatre continued to develop and thrive in the shadow of the Great White Way. The American Negro Theatre was formed by playwright/director Abram Hill, Frederick O'Neal, and several members of the disbanded Rose McClendon Players. Moving into the basement of the 135th Street Library, its first production was a revival of Abram Hill's satire of black middle-class pretensions, *On Striver's Row*. Subsequent productions included a controversial black adaptation of Phillip Yordan's *Anna Lucasta*, which revealed a high degree of ensemble execution in the performances of Hilda Simms, Frederick O'Neal, Alice Childress, Alvin Childress, Earle Hyman, and Herbert Henry. At the same time, a group of writers including Theodore Ward, Powell Lindsay, George Norford, Theodore Browne, and Owen Dodson created the Negro Playwrights Company. Its initial production was Theodore Ward's *The Big White Fog*, which had earlier received a good deal of critical attention in the Chicago Unit of the Federal Theatre Project.

The social climate had become intense following the end of World War II, and efforts toward integration had begun to gain favor in the objectives of many black theatre groups. Despite the violence that prevailed against blacks and the constant harassment from the FBI's pursuit of "un-American" activities in Harlem, a retrograde sense of ambivalence found its way into the newly developed projects. As illustrated by *Anna Lucasta*, a tendency to define the black experience through the safe adaptation of popularly produced white works had created much internal dissension within the ranks of the Black Theatre community, which ultimately stalled the growth of the movement.

Entering into the fifties, the Black Theatre Movement in Harlem became inactive. Ironically, there was more opportunity for blacks to work on Broadway—in plays such as Joshua Logan's adaptation of Chekhov's *Cherry Orchard*, *The Wisteria Trees*, or Carson McCullers *The Member of the Wedding*, with its reconfiguration of the noble servant—than in Harlem. Though underemployed, these actors worked Broadway, while the theatre scene uptown became dormant, with unemployed actors, writers, directors, and technicians. As a result, a group of concerned theatre artists—including Maxwell Glanville, Alice Childress, Ruth Jett, Sylvester Leaks, and William Coleman—formed the Council on the Harlem Theatre. Their objective was to create a cooperative relationship among the few remaining theatre groups in Harlem, which would allow them to share resources—actors, scenery, mailing lists—as well as coordinate production schedules to avoid conflicts. They also agreed to promote works that reflected the African-American cultural experience. One of the successful productions emerging from the new mood of cooperation was Alice Childress's adaptation of Langston Hughes's "Simple Speaks His Mind", which had been a popular column in black newspapers. The new work, which characterized the popular folk hero raconteur Jesse B. Simple, was entitled *Just A Little Simple*, and was enthusiastically received in Harlem at the Club Baron in 1950.

In 1951, the Apollo Theatre decided to produce two plays, *Detective Story* and

Rain. Sidney Poitier, who had just returned from Hollywood where he was featured with Canada Lee in *Cry, the Beloved Country*—a moving film about black life in South Africa—was asked to perform the lead role in *Detective Story*. It was a time when even Poitier was struggling for artistic survival, so he accepted the role despite the apparent contradiction involved in an empathetic presentation of the police during a time when the community was constantly under siege from police brutality. The play had a short life, leaving Poitier the opportunity to open a small barbecue restaurant, "Ribs and Ruff," to support himself. He worked extremely hard in-between jobs. His partner, Johnny Newton, worked the day shift, and Poitier worked the midnight shift. His career as an actor seemed to be wavering until he finally received a call from Hollywood to return for a major role in *The Blackboard Jungle*.

In 1951, while Poitier, like many other actors, was trying to keep a footing in the theatre, William Branch was having his play, *A Medal for Willie* produced at the Club Baron. The work received critical acclaim and provoked a great deal of controversy among some blacks, who objected to certain aspects of black life being revealed for public scrutiny. Included in the cast were Clarice Taylor, Helen Martin, Julian Mayfield, Kenneth Mannigault, and Eli Wallach. The set designer for the production was Roger Furman.

In 1952, Julian Mayfield and Maxwell Glanville formed an independent production company to produce three one-act plays: *A World Full of Men* and *The Other Foot* were written by Mayfield, and *Alice in Wonder*—also the collective title for the venture— was the first play written by Ossie Davis. The effort was supported by a small donation from William Marshall, who had just completed the Hollywood film *Lydia Bailey*, and by Poitier, who allowed his "Ribs and Ruff" restaurant, which was frequented by many people in show business, to be a site for the sale of tickets. The show opened at the Elks Community Theatre and boasted a cast that included Ed Cambridge and Ruby Dee. Vocalist/actor Leon Bibb was the set designer. The community was back to work with a renewed commitment to the collective interests of both the audience and the artist.

Broadway loomed brighter for blacks in 1953 with the production of Louis Peterson's *Take A Giant Step*, which featured Louis Gossett, Jr. While the play received warm reviews, its revival off-Broadway in 1956 at the Jan Hus House was even more glowing, and featured a stellar cast which included Bill Gunn, Godfrey Cambridge, Frances Foster, and Juanita Bethea. Off-Broadway also had the Village Mews Theatre, which provided opportunities for black theatre artists to work during the mid-fifties. Its policy of casting plays irrespective of color or ethnicity antedates recent attempts to introduce into regional theatres in America the concept of non-traditional casting. Alice Childress's *Trouble in Mind* was one of several works by black authors which received fully mounted productions at the Village Mews.

In spite of the many plays that were being developed away from Broadway by black writers, there were still black artists who continued the convention of adapting existing American classics—such as actor/director Luther James, who produced a Loften Mitchell black adaptation of Steinbeck's *Of Mice and Men* at a Greenwich Village cabaret with a cast that included Charles Gordone, Bill Gunn, Howard Augusta, and Clayton Corbin. However, the fifties ended with the production of a modern American classic penned by a black author: Lorraine Hansberry's *A Raisin in the Sun*. The Broadway cast included many of the luminaries who would contribute invaluably to the continued evolvement of the Black Theatre Movement in the sixties: Sidney Poitier (replaced later by Ossie Davis), Ruby Dee, Claudia McNeil, Diana Sands, Ivan Dixon, Louis Gossett, Jr., Lonne Elder III, Douglas Turner Ward, and director Lloyd Richards. *A Raisin in the Sun* is a work which is quintessentially American in style and content, and it generated a renewed enthusiasm within the black artist community to pursue the challenge of playwriting, as opposed to concentrating exclusively on performing skills.

It is interesting that the writing of several actors has made an impact on the literature of the Black Theatre Movement: Ossie Davis's *Purlie Victorious*, Lonne Elder III's *Ceremonies in Dark Old Men*, Samm Art Williams's *Home*, Philip Hayes Dean's *Sty of the Blind Pig*, Charles Gordone's Pulitzer Prize-winning play, *No Place to Be Somebody*, Bill Gunn's *Black Picture Show*, and Douglas Turner Ward's two one-act works that led to the formation of the Negro Ensemble Company, *Happy Ending* and *Day of Absence*. The impetus for the Black Theatre Movement, however, did not come directly from the performing community. It was the result of a groundswell of Black Nationalism throughout the country which had been precipitated by social activists and political radicals who used the theatre as a mode of collective communication. The sheer force of the rhetoric awakened an entirely new audience to the emergence of a newly informed black aesthetic which formulated alternatives to Euro-American tastes. The new works would be entertaining, yet instructive. In the process, the works sought to achieve a new ethnocentric focus by drawing symbols and language from the residue of African-American folk culture. Rather than the static exposition of black life through melodramatic social realism, the new works would seek to have the stylistic, non-linear freedom of jazz, and the poetic eloquence of folk narratives. The resulting products of the new aesthetic and political focus produced an inclination toward examining the complexities of the black experience through abstract logic rather than over-simplified, slice-of-life dramas. The direct beneficiaries of the ethnocentric thrust of the Black Art Movement in the sixties were the theatre artist themselves; it allowed them an opportunity to work without compromising their personal or collective ethnic visions. Black culture had been reaffirmed as in no other period in African-American history, cutting across class lines to embrace the collective consciousness.

Arguably, Jean Genet's *The Blacks*, an allegorical work written by a French sociopath who identified with the oppressed classes of the world, paved the way for channeling the new social, political, and artistic focus of Black Theatre. The work was produced in 1961 at the St. Marks Playhouse in East Greenwich Village during a time when the Civil Rights Movement was turning the corner of civil disobedience and heading for direct confrontation. Genet's assault on European colonialism held the emotional resonance of racism for the black American cast, thereby giving the work a sense of incendiary urgency that proved to be successful. The long run of the play allowed the cast to be recycled several times, thus providing opportunities to showcase the talents of several actors who would become major forces in the world of American entertainment. Among them were Cicely Tyson, James Earl Jones, Louis Gossett, Jr., Roscoe Lee Browne, and Maya Angelou, to name but a few.

During the 1963-64 season, several events would impact on the direction of Black Theatre. Far away from the Great White Way, the Free Southern Theatre, in response to Civil Rights activism, was organized in New Orleans by John O'Neal and Gilbert Moses. Its mission was to tour southern black communities with established American and European plays. Though somewhat contradictory to the mood of Black Nationalism, the works were offered free to many appreciative black audiences throughout the South, with the most popular response being reserved for Beckett's *Waiting for Godot*.

Meanwhile, closer to the lights of Broadway, Adrienne Kennedy's surrealistic dream-play, *Funnyhouse of A Negro*, was produced by the Edward Albee Workshop in Greenwich Village. The work owns an introspective poetic style that would be emulated by many women dramatists in the future. The workshop also produced *Dutchman*, a work by Amiri Baraka (LeRoi Jones) which stunned New York audiences with its social metaphors of sexual-racial aggression proffered through symbolist drama. Baraka, a poet who would influence the voicing of poets for the next two generations, had turned to dramaturgy as a vehicle to express the dialectics of Black Art and Black Nationalism. Subsequently, his two one-act plays, *The Slave* and *The Toilet* were produced at the St. Marks Playhouse. These works vaulted Baraka to Harlem in 1965, where he joined with Larry Neal in establishing the Black Arts Repertory Theatre to advance the dialectics of his ideology from a black community base. While this was taking place, members of the Free Southern Theatre, including Gil Moses, Roscoe Orman, Denise Nicholas, and John O'Neal, began to urge the organization away from its white orientation and toward a theatre that explored black folk life, an experience that had long been ignored by the American mainstream.

Soon after, Robert Hooks and Gerald Krone produced Douglas Turner Ward's two plays, *Happy Ending* and *Day of Absence*, at the St. Marks Playhouse—which in 1967 would become the permanent home of the Negro Ensemble Company, under the artistic leadership of Ward and the managerial guidance of Krone and Hooks. Many actors benefited from the stable presence of this nationally and internationally acclaimed company; and the NEC was an extremely vital writer's theatre, credited with having introduced more important writers of African descent to the commercial theatre than any institutional theatre ever created in America or abroad. Among the works nurtured by NEC are Lonne Elder III's *Ceremonies in Dark Old Men*, Joseph Walker's *River Niger*, and Charles Fuller's *A Soldier's Play*.

Though the NEC, endowed with a wealth of professional talent, wore the mantel of a national theatre, other theatre groups began to come into existence uptown, in Harlem. Robert McBeth formed the New Lafayette Theatre with Ed Bullins as playwright-in-residence, but despite the emergence of another fine playwright, Richard Wesley, the operation more or less limited itself to revolutionary exercises. Roger Furman remained a resilient tutorial and creative force in Harlem with the New Heritage Repertory Theatre. Ernie McClintock organized the Afro-American Studio Theatre, where he used black life styles as the reference point for teaching acting to local youths.

The National Black Theatre was created by Barbara Ann Teer to investigate rituals emanating from the religious experience of black folk. Playwright Garland Lee Thompson had created the Frank Silvera Writer's Workshop to hold seminars and review works-in-progress for developing playwrights. While these Harlem-based groups diligently focused their energies on the cultural enhancement of the community, Vinnette Carroll, with no less empathy for the Harlem goals, organized the Urban Arts Corps, where she trained black and Puerto Rican young people for careers in the professional theatre. In the process, she was able to develop Broadway-bound works, including Micki Grant's pop-musical *Don't Bother Me I Can't Cope*, and the gospel musical *Your Arms Too Short to Box with God*.

In the seventies, the Great White Way began to acknowledge the presence of black producers. After a successful run at Joseph Papp's Public Theatre, Charles Gordone's *No Place to Be Somebody* was produced on Broadway by Ashton Springer, a Harlem resident who, having no former producing experience, was able to capitalize on his acumen for business. The Broadway success was capped by a Pulitzer Prize for Charles Gordone. Other works subsequently produced by Springer included the musical *Bubbling Brown Sugar*, which introduced director/choreographer Billie Wilson to the legitimate stage, and featured Josephine Premise, Joseph Attles, and Avon Long. That work was followed by a black adaptation of *Guys and Dolls*.

Ken Harper, a journeyman actor, conceived and successfully produced *The Wiz*—but had to overcome the predictably negative critical response to the black adaptation of one of America's favorite fables, *The Wizard of Oz*, through direct appeal to the black metropolitan community. Not only did the musical survive, it became a bona fide success by commercial standards. The work featured Stephanie Mills and Dee Dee Bridgewater, but also revealed the genius of

Charlie Smalls's music, the wizardry of George Faison's choreography, and the whimsical magic of Geoffrey Holder's costume designs.

Among the independent producers, Woodie King, Jr. remains unrivaled in terms of the number of projects he has brought to both Broadway and off-Broadway. Operating from under the institutional umbrella of the New Federal Theatre at the Henry Street Settlement on the Lower East Side of Manhattan, King has showcased a wide range of minority playwrights, including the early work of Asian American David Henry Hwang. Several of the works showcased at Henry Street benefited from a special arrangement with Joe Papp at the Public Theatre, which picked up successful productions for extended commercial runs. Such was the case with Ed Bullins's *The Taking of Miss Janie*, and Ntozake Shange's *For Colored Girls Who Have Considered Suicide/When the Rainbow Is Enuf*, which played on Broadway.

An early association with Ron Milner in Detroit led to a relationship that allowed King to introduce several of Milner's works to the commercial stage, including *Who's Got His Own* (1964); *The Warning—A Theme for Linda* (1969, part of a program of one-act plays that included Baraka's *Great Goodness of Life*, Ben Caldwell's *Prayer Meeting or the First Militant Preacher*, and Bullin's *The Gentleman Caller*, presented under the collective title of *Black Quartet*); *What the Wine-Sellers Buy* (1973); and, following a national tour that led to Broadway in 1988, *Check Mates*, featuring Denzel Washington. Anticipating the fact that the Black Theatre might have a difficult time surviving the commercial pressures of New York, King and a long-time associate, actress/director Shauneille Perry, formed the National Black Touring Circuit in order to create a vehicle for wider dissemination of the plays, and sustain the Black Theatre Movement outside of New York.

Other support structures for the Black Theatre Movement include the Audience Development Committee (Audelco), a service organization headed by Vivian Robinson which was established to develop new audiences and stimulate community interest in the arts. Audelco has played a very significant role in the efforts of commercial as well as non-profit theatres to generate audiences for various productions. Another support group, the Black Theatre Alliance, provided black theatre groups in New York with an administrative base to promote Black Theatre throughout the city. Formed in 1973, its membership included—in addition to those community based companies mentioned earlier—the Brownsville Laboratory Theatre, the Afro-American Total Theatre (later known as the Richard Allen Cultural Center), the Bed-Stuy Theatre, the Cornbread Players, Black Vibrations, the Demi-Gods, the Weusi Kuumba Troupe, the East River Players, and Voices Inc.

In the meantime, and perhaps most importantly for its continued presence as a legitimate alternative to the conventional commercial theatre, the Black Theatre Movement has proliferated to the regionals. While Karamu House, formed in Cleveland, Ohio in 1916, is the oldest of the regional theatre, the

1989 Black Theatre Festival at the North Carolina Black Repertory in Winston-Salem was a testament to nationwide participation in the dissemination of Black Theatre. Some of the theatres invited to the festival included the Oakland Ensemble; the Theatre Workshop of Louisville; the Watts Repertory Theatre; the Black Theatre Troupe of Phoenix; the Arkansas Repertory of Little Rock; Rights and Reasons of Providence; Actors Inc. Theatre Production of Indianapolis; the Black Experience Ensemble of Albany, New York; the Bullins Memorial Theatre of Emoryville, California; the Black Street USA Puppet Theatre of Los Angeles; the Blues City Cultural Center for the Performing Arts of Memphis; the Creekside Players of Dayton, Ohio; the Eden Theatre of Denver; Theatre International of Philadelphia; the Arena Stage of Baltimore; the Kuumba Theatre of Chicago; and the Los Angeles Inner-City Cultural Center, which is in the process, as of this writing, of purchasing the Ivar Theatre in Hollywood, located next to the Huntington Hartford Theatre.

This wider dispersal provides opportunities for Black writers to develop their works—as have August Wilson at Penumbra Theatre in Minneapolis/St. Paul, Pearl Cleage at Just Us Theatre in Atlanta, Georgia, and George Wolfe at the Cross Roads Theatre in New Brunswick, New Jersey—and for black theatre artists of all kinds. Black Theatre is clearly alive and well in America; it exists as a vital contribution to American cultural life, no longer in the shadow of the Great White Way.

Paul Carter Harrison

For further discussion of the history of the Black Theatre in America, readers may consult the following books:

Fabrea, Genevieve. *Drumbeats, Masks, and Metaphor*. Cambridge: Harvard University Press, 1983.

Harrison, Paul Carter. *The Drama of Nommo*. New York: Grove Press, 1972.

Mitchell, Loften. *Black Drama: The Story of the American Negro in the Theatre*. New York: Hawthorne Books, 1967.

Williams, Mance. *Black Theatre in the 1960s and 1970s: A Historical-Critical Analysis of the Movement*. Westport: Greenwood Press, 1985.

Images from the Black Theatre
1957 – 1984

Dark of the Moon, 1957—Cicely Tyson, Clarence Williams III, Roscoe Lee Browne, Louise Stubbs,
Richard Ward, Lea Scott; with Vinnette Carroll directing. (Written by Howard Richardson and
William Berney. Produced by the YMCA Drama Guild in association with the Little Theatre Players
and the Harlem Showcase at the Little Theatre, New York.)

Moon on a Rainbow Shawl, 1962—Robert Earl Jones, Cicely Tyson, James Earl Jones, Vinnette Carroll, Ellen Holly, Bill Gunn, Melvin Stewart, Kelly Marie Berry. (Written by Errol John. Directed by George Roy Hill. Produced by Kermit Bloomgarden and Harry Joe Brown, Jr. at the East 11th Street Theater, New York.)

Black Nativity, 1961—Alex Bradford interacting with the audience. (Written by Langston Hughes. Directed by Vinnette Carroll. Produced by Michael R. Santangelo, Barbra Griner, and Gary Kramer at the 41st Street Theater, New York.)

The Grass Harp, 1961—Ernestine McClendon, later the first black actor's
agent. (Written by Truman Capote. Directed by Vinnette Carroll. Produced
by the Equity Library Theatre at the Lenox Hill Playhouse, New York.)

Talking to You, from *Two by Saroyan*, 1961—Alvin Ailey. (Written by William Saroyan. Directed by Arthur Storch. Produced by Shelly Gordon and Barry Gordon at the East End Theatre, New York.)

Desperate Hours, 1962—Sammy Davis, Jr. (Written by Joseph Hayes. Directed by Lloyd Richards. Produced by Henry T. Weinstein and Laurence Feldman in association with Will Mastin at the Mineola Playhouse, Mineola, New York.)

The Blacks, 1961—Michelle Nichols, Lincoln Kilpatrick, Helen Martin, Louis Gossett, Jr., Ethel Ayler, Clebert Ford. (Written by Jean Genet. Translated by Bernard Frechtman. Directed by Gene Frankel. Produced by Sidney Bernstein, George Edgar, and Andre Gregory by arrangement with Geraldine Lust at the St. Marks Playhouse, New York.)

The Blacks, 1961—Roxie Roker, Raymond St. Jaques, Lex Monson, Louis Gossett, Jr., Louise Stubbs, Cynthia Belgrave, Cicely Tyson, Helen Martin, Roscoe Lee Browne.

The Blacks, 1962—Louis Gossett, Jr., Brunetta Barnett, Ethel Ayler.

The Blacks, 1963—Martin Luther King and Coretta Scott King visiting backstage with Bobby Dean Hooks and Louise Stubbs.

The Blacks, 1964—Marlene Warfield, Billy Dee Williams, Louise Stubbs.

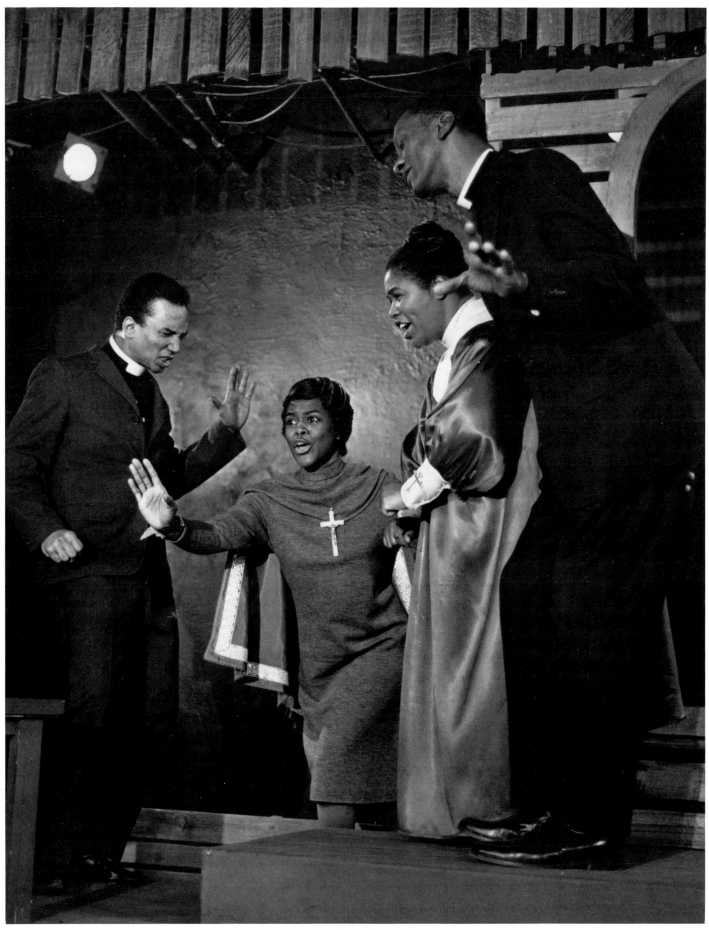

Trumpets of the Lord, 1963—Al Freeman, Jr., Cicely Tyson, Theresa Merritt, and Lex Monson at dress rehearsal. (Adapted by Vinnette Carroll from James Weldon Johnson's *God's Trombone*. Directed by Donald McKayle. Musical direction by Howard Roberts. Produced by Theodore Mann in association with Will B. Sandler at the Astor Place Playhouse, New York.)

Trumpets of the Lord, 1963—Cicely Tyson.

Blue Boy in Black, 1963—Cicely Tyson. (Written by Edmund White. Directed and produced by Ashley Feinstein at the Masque Theater, New York.)

Mr. Johnson, 1963—James Earl Jones. (Written by Norman Rosten, based on a novel by Joyce Cary. Directed by Tom Greenwald. Produced by the Equity Library Theatre at the Master Theatre, New York.)

Ballad for Bimshire, 1963—Charles Moore and Cast. (Book by Irving Burgie and Loften Mitchell. Lyrics and music by Irving "Lord Burgess" Burgie. Directed by Ed Cambridge. Produced by Ossie Davis, Bernard Waltzer and Page Productions at the Mayfair Theatre, New York.)

Ballad for Bimshire, 1963—Miriam Burton, Frederick O'Neal.

The Blood Knot, 1964—Allen Miller, Douglas Turner. (Written by Athol Fugard. Directed by John Berry. Produced by Sidney Bernstein and Lucille Lortel Productions, Inc. at the Cricket Theatre, New York.)

The Slave, 1964—Nan Martin, Al Freeman, Jr. (A one-act play presented with *The Toilet*. Written by LeRoi Jones [Amiri Baraka]. Directed by Leo Garen. Produced by Leo Garen and Stan Swerdlow in association with Gene Persson and Rita Fredricks at the St. Marks Playhouse, New York.)

The Toilet, 1964—Norman Bush, Hampton Clanton, Garry Bolling, Bostic Van Felton, Tony Hudson, D'Urville Martin, Jamie Sanchez, Antonio Fargas, Walter Jones, James Spruill, Gary Haynes. (Presented as a one-act play with *The Slave*. Written by LeRoi Jones [Amiri Baraka]. Directed by Leo Garen. Produced by Leo Garen and Stan Swerdlow in association with Gene Persson and Rita Fredricks at the St. Marks Playhouse, New York.)

The Premise, 1965—Jo Ann Lecompte, Al Freeman, Jr., Diana Sands. (Integrated improvisational theatre, with material by the performers. Produced by Theodore Flicker at The Premise, New York.)

Othello, 1964—James Earl Jones and Julienne Marie. (Written by William Shakespeare. Directed by Gladys Vaughan. Produced by the New York Shakespeare Festival at Central Park, New York.)

Jericho-Jim Crow, 1964—Gilbert Price, Hilda Harris. (Written by Langston Hughes. Directed by Alvin Ailey and William Hairston. Produced by Greenwich Players, Inc., in coordination with CORE, NAACP, and SNCC at The Sanctuary, New York.)

Happy Ending, 1965—Robert Hooks, Douglas Turner, Esther Rolle, Frances Foster. (Written by Douglas Turner Ward. Directed by Philip Meister. Produced by Robert Hooks, Inc., at the St. Marks Playhouse, New York.)

Day of Absence, 1965—Barbara Ann Teer. (Written by Douglas Turner Ward. Directed by Philip Meister. Produced by Robert Hooks, Inc., at the St. Marks Playhouse, New York.)

Lorenzaccio, 1965—Cliff Frazier. (Written by Alfred De Musset. Directed by Osvaldo Riofrancos. Produced by the Equity Library Theatre at the Master Theatre, New York.)

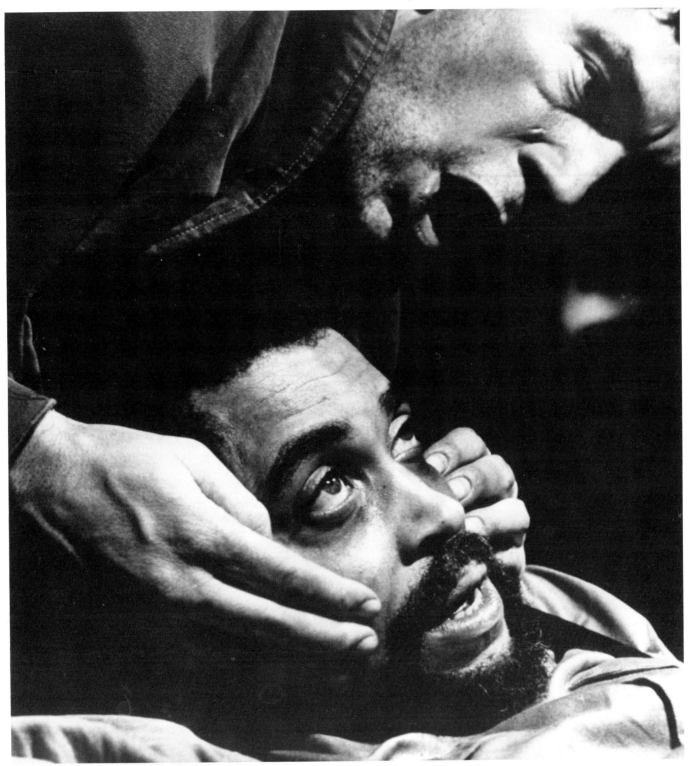

Baal, 1966—James Earl Jones, Mitch Ryan. (Written by Bertolt Brecht. Adapted by Eric Bentley and Martin Esslin. Directed by Gladys Vaughan. Produced by Circle in the Square Theatre in association with Theodore Mann and Paul Libin at the Martinique Theatre, New York.)

Above: *The Prodigal Son*, 1965—Glory Van Scott, Philip A. Stamps. (Written by Langston Hughes. Directed by Vinnette Carroll. Produced by Landau, Holt, and Stein at the Greenwhich Mews Theater, New York.)

Below: *A Funny Thing Happened on the Way to the Forum*, 1965—Arnold Soboloff, Godfrey Cambridge. (Written by Burt Shevelove and Larry Gelbart. Music and lyrics by Stephen Sondheim. Produced by Oakdale Music Theatre, Wallingford Music Theater, Ben Segak, Bob Hall, and Burton "Buster" Barnoff.)

Big Time Buck White, 1968—Arnold Williams, David Moody (interacting with audience), Van Kirksey, Dick Williams. (Written by Joseph Dolan Tuotti. Directed by Dick Williams. Produced by Zev Buffman, Ron Rich, and Leonard Grant at the Village South Theatre, New York.)

Daddy Goodness, 1967-68 season—Moses Gunn, Denise Nicholas, Judyann Jonsson, Rosalind Cash. (Written by Richard Wright and Louis Sapin. Directed by Douglas Turner Ward. Produced by the Negro Ensemble Company at the St. Marks Playhouse, New York.)

The Summer of the Seventeenth Doll, 1968—Frances Foster, Norman Bush, Moses Gunn, Esther Rolle, Clarice Taylor. (Written by Ray Lawler. Directed by Edmund Cambridge. Produced by the Negro Ensemble Company at the St. Marks Playhouse, New York.)

The Blood Knot, 1968—Louis Gossett, Jr., Nicholas Coster.

To Be Young, Gifted and Black, 1969—Rita Gardner, Cicely Tyson, Janet League. (Adapted from "The World of Lorraine Hansberry" by Robert Nemiroff. Directed by Gene Frankel. Produced by Harry Belafonte, Chiz Shultz, and Edgar Lansbury, in association with Robert Nemiroff at the Cherry Lane Theatre, New York.)

Carry Me Back to Morningside Heights, 1968—Cicely
Tyson, Louis Gossett, Jr. (Written by Robert Alan
Aurthur. Directed by Sidney Poitier. Produced by
Saint Subber and Harold Loeb at the John Golden
Theatre, New York.)

Carry Me Back to Morningside Heights, 1968—David Steinberg, Cicely Tyson, Louis Gossett, Jr., Diane Ladd, Johnny Brown, Sidney Poitier (director).

God is a (Guess What?), 1968—Judyann Jonsson, Rosalind Cash, Allie Woods, Hattie Winston, Julius Harris, unidentified. (Written by Ray McIver. Directed by Michael A. Schultz. Music by Coleridge-Taylor Perkinson. Choreography by Louis Johnson. Produced by the Negro Ensemble Company at the St. Marks Playhouse, New York.)

Slave Ship, 1969—Lee Chamberlin, C. Robert Scott. (Written by LeRoi Jones [Amiri Baraka]. Music by Archie Shepp and Gilbert Moses. Directed by Gilbert Moses. Produced by Chelsea Theatre Center in association with Woodie King, Jr. at the Brooklyn Academy of Music, New York.)

House of Flowers, 1968—Josephine Premice. (Book by Truman Capote. Music by Harold Arlen. Lyrics by Truman Capote and Mrs. Arlen. Directed by Joseph Hardy. Produced by Saint Subber by special arrangement with Lucille Lortel Productions at the Theatre de Lys, New York.)

Ceremonies in Dark Old Men, 1968-69 season—Jerry Bell, Glynn Thurman, Rosalind Cash, Godfrey Cambridge. (Written by Lonne Elder III. Directed by Edmund Cambridge. Produced by the Negro Ensemble Company. Photograph from the television version of the play.)

Rosencrantz and Guildenstern Are Dead, 1969—Clebert Ford, John Church. (Written by Tom Stoppard. Directed by Jacqueline Britton. Produced by Producing Managers Company at the Playhouse Theatre, Deleware.)

Passing Through From Exotic Places, 1969—Peter DeAnda, Robert Loggia, Vincent Gardenia, Tresa Hughes. (Three one-act plays written by Ronald Ribman. Directed by Eugene Lesser. Produced by Kleinman-Reiss Productions, Capricorn Company, and Studley-Traub at the Sheridan Square Playhouse, New York.)

Above: *The Ofay Watcher*, 1969—Cleavon Little, Billie Allen, Terry Kiser. (Written by Frank Cucci. Directed by Jerry Adler. Produced by Harlan P. Kleiman, Jeffrey C. Reiss, and Patrick MacNamara.)

Below: *The Reckoning*, 1969—Douglas Turner, Lester Rawlins, Jeanette DuBois. (Written by Douglas Turner Ward. Directed by Michael A. Schultz. Produced by Hooks Productions Inc. in cooperation with the Negro Ensemble Company at the St. Marks Playhouse, New York.)

Above: *Contribution*, 1970—Claudia McNeil, Louise Stubbs. (Presented with *Shoes* and *Plantation* as "Contributions." Written by Ted Shine. Directed by Moses Gunn. Produced by Jonathan Burrows in association with Ruthe Feldman and Ken Gaston Productions at the Tambellini's Gate Theater, New York.)

Below: *Shoes*, 1970—Donald Griffith, Charles Grant, Jim Jones, Stanley Greene. (Presented with *Plantation* and *Contribution* as "Contributions." Written by Ted Shine. Directed by Moses Gunn. Produced by Jonathan Burrows in association with Ruthe Feldman and Ken Gaston Productions at Tambellini's Gate Theater, New York.)

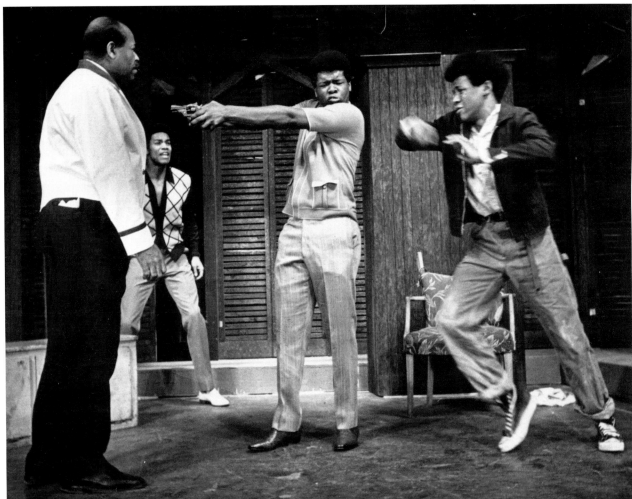

The Harangues, 1969-70 season—Julius W. Harris, Elliot Cuker, William Jay, Douglas Turner, Linda Carlson. (Two one-act plays written by Joseph A. Walker. Music by Dorothy A. Dinroe. Directed by Israel Hicks. Produced by the Negro Ensemble Company at the St. Marks Playhouse, New York.)

Slow Dance on the Killing Ground, 1965—Billy Dee Williams. (Written by William Hanley. Directed by David Marlin-Jones. Produced by the Washington Theatre Club.)

The Me Nobody Knows, 1970—Melanie Henderson, Jose Fernandez, Irene Cara. (Spoken text written by children ages 7 to 18 attending New York City public schools, and edited by Stephen M. Joseph. Music by Gary Friedman. Lyrics by Will Holt. Original idea by Herb Schapiro. Directed by Robert Livingston. Produced by Jeff Britton and Sagittarius Productions at the Orpheum Theater, New York.)

The Me Nobody Knows, 1970—Gerri Dean, Northern J. Calloway, Melanie Henderson.

The Dream on Monkey Mountain, 1971—Roscoe Lee Browne, Antonio Fargas, Robert Jackson.
(Written by Derek Walcott. Directed by Michael A. Schultz. Produced by the Negro Ensemble
Company at the St. Marks Playhouse, New York.)

Ain't Supposed to Die A Natural Death, 1971—Dick Williams, Gloria Edwards. (Book, lyrics, and music by Melvin Van Peebles. Directed by Gilbert Moses. Produced by Eugene V. Wolsk, Charles Blackwell, Emanuel Azenberg, and Robert Malina at the Ethel Barrymore Theater, New York.)

Above: *Day of Absence*, 1970—Allie Woods, Norman Bush, Bill Duke, Arthur French, William Jay. (Written and directed by Douglas Turner Ward. Revival produced by the Negro Ensemble Company at the St. Marks Playhouse, New York.)

Below: *Ain't Supposed to Die A Natural Death*, 1971—Jimmy Hayeson, Madge Wells, Carl Gordon, Barbara Alston, Lauren Jones, Clebert Ford.

The Sty of the Blind Pig, 1971—Moses Gunn, Frances Foster, Adolph Caesar, Clarice Taylor. (Written by Philip Hayes Dean. Directed by Shauneille Perry. Produced by the Negro Ensemble Company at the St. Marks Theatre, New York.)

Behold! Cometh the Vanderkellans, 1971—Graham Brown, Carl Byrd, Roxie Roker, Robert Christian, Frances Foster. (Written by William Wellington Mackey. Directed by Edmund Cambridge. Produced by Woodie King Associates, Russell Price, Ida Epps, and the National Center for Afro-American Artists at Theater de Lys, New York.)

Above: *Please Don't Cry and Say No*, 1972—David Downing, Janet League. (Written by Townsend Brewster. Music by Dorothy A. Dinroe. Directed by Philip Taylor. Produced by Sally Sears and Primavera Productions, Ltd. at Circle in the Square, New York.)

Below: *Ladies in Waiting*, 1973—Juanita Bethea, Yolanda Karr, Pearl Faith, Anna Horsford, Saundra Kelly. (Written by Peter DeAnda. Directed by Shauneille Perry. Produced by the Black Theatre Alliance Festival and the New Federal Theatre.)

Lost in the Stars, 1972—Brock Peters, Gilbert Price, Margaret Cowie. (Words by Maxwell Anderson. Based on Alan Paton's novel *Cry, the Beloved Country*. Music by Kurt Weill. Directed by Gene Frankel. Choreography and musical staging by Louis Johnson. Produced by Roger L. Stevens and Diana Shumlin at the Imperial Theater, New York.)

The River Niger, 1972—Douglas Turner Ward, Roxie Roker. (Written by Joseph A. Walker. Directed by Douglas Turner Ward. Produced by the Negro Ensemble Company at St. Marks Playhouse, New York.)

Above: *La Femme Noir*, 1974—Novella Nelson (director) and
Company. (Written by Edgar White. Produced by the New York
Shakespeare Festival.)

Below: *Great MacDaddy*, 1974—Charles Weldon, Hattie Winston,
Howard Porter, Sati Jamal, Adolph Caeser. (Written by Paul Carter
Harrison. Directed by Douglas Turner Ward. Music by Coleridge-
Taylor Perkinson. Choreography by Dianne McIntyre. Produced
by the Negro Ensemble Company at the St. Marks Playhouse.)

Dudder Love, 1972—Garrett Morris, Bill Cobbs, LeeRoy Giles, Norman Jacob, Alfonso Akeela, Joyce Griffen, Vanessa Gilder. (Written by Walter Jones. Directed by Bill Duke. Produced by the New Federal Theatre at the Henry Street Settlement.)

The Prodigal Sister, 1974—Neal Tate, Micki Grant, Shauneille Perry, and cast: Paula Desmond, Francis Salisbury, Esther Brown, Ethel Beatty, Leonard Jackson, Louise Stubbs, Saundra McClain, Kirk Kirksey, Frank Carey, Joyce Griffen, Victor Willis, Judy Dearing, Yolande Graves, Rael Lamb, Larry Lowe. (Book and lyrics by J.E. Franklin. Music and lyrics by Micki Grant. Directed by Shauneille Perry. Musical Direction by Neal Tate. Choreography by Rod Rodgers. Produced by Woodie King, Jr. at the Theater de Lys, New York.)

Cotillon, 1975—(Front:) Joyce Griffiths, Taurean Blacque, (Back:) Hank Frazier, Zaida Coles.
(Written by John O. Killens. Directed by Allie Woods. Produced by Woodie King, Jr. at the New
Federal Theatre, New York.)

The Taking of Miss Janie, 1975—Cast. (Written by Ed Bullins. Directed by Gilbert Moses. Produced by the New York Shakespeare Festival in association with Woodie King, Jr. and the New Federal Theatre at the Mitzi E. Newhouse Theater, New York. Winner of the Drama Critics Award for 1975.)

THREE PLAYS ABOUT BESSIE SMITH

Above: *Bessie Smith, Empress of the Blues*, 1981—Jerry Sheldon, Allen Taylor, Yvette Erwin, Ebony JoAnn Pickney, Clebert Ford. (Written by Ed Shockley. Directed by Charles Turner. Produced by the Frank Silvera Writer's Workshop. Opposite, top: *Champeen*, 1983—Sandra Reaves-Phillips. (Book, music, and lyrics by Melvin Van Peebles. Directed by Melvin Van Peebles. Produced by Woodie King, Jr. and the New Federal Theatre at the Henry Street Settlement. Opposite, bottom: *Me & Bessie*, 1975—Linda Hopkins and musicians. (Written by Will Holt. Concept by Linda Hopkins. Directed by Robert Greenwald. Produced by Norman Kean in association with Lee Apostoveris, Center Theatre Group/Mark Taper Forum, at the Edison Theatre, New York.)

Sisyphus and the Blue Eyed Cyclops, 1975—David Cornell, Morgan Freeman, Jr., Robin Braxton, Edythe Davis, Brent Jennings. (Written and Directed by Garland Lee Thompson. Produced by the Frank Silvera Writer's Workshop.)

Bubbling Brown Sugar, 1976—Joseph Attles, Vivian Reed, Josephine Premice, Avon Long. (Book by
Loften Mitchell, based on a concept by Rosetta LeNoire. Directed by Robert N. Cooper. Musical direction
by Danny Holgate. Choreography and musical staging by Billy Wilson. Produced by J. Lloyd Grant,
Richard Bell, Robert M. Cooper, and Ashton Springer in association with Moe Septee, Inc. at the
ANTA Theatre, New York.)

The Square Root of Soul, 1976—Adolph Caeser. (Text from an anthology of verse by black writers, conceived and adapted by Adolph Caeser. Directed by Perry Shwartz. Produced by the Negro Ensemble Company at the Theater de Lys, New York.)

Pappa B' on the D' Train, 1976—Joan Hart and Bob Molock. (Written by Garland Lee Thompson. Directed by LeRoy Giles. Produced by the Frank Silvera Writer's Workshop.)

Paul Robeson, 1977—James Earl Jones. (Written by Philip Hayes Dean. Directed by Lloyd Richards. Produced by Don Gregory at the Lunt-Fontanne Theater, New York.)

Survival, 1977—Seth Sibanda, Fana David Kekana, Selaelo Dan Maredi, Themba Ntinga. (A South African musical in two acts written by the cast. Co-authored and originally directed by Mshengu. Additional staging by Dean Irby. Produced by Clyde Kuemmerle in association with the Negro Ensemble Company.)

For Colored Girls Who Have Considered Suicide/When the Rainbow is Enuf, 1978—Gloria Calomee, Marilyn Johnson, Alfre Woodward, Lynn Whitfield. (Written by Ntozake Shange. Directed by Oz Scott. Produced by Woodie King, Jr. in association with the Los Angeles Company.)

The Basic Training of Pavlo Hummel, 1977—Joe Fields, Al Pacino. (Written by David Rabe. Directed by David Wheeler. Produced by Moe Septee, Carmen F. Zollo, and the Theatre Company of Boston at the Longacre Theatre, Boston.)

Incarnations of Reverend Goode Blaque Dresse, 1978—Dave Connell, Charles Brown, Akin Babatunde.
(Written by Garland Lee Thompson. Directed by Dean Irby. Produced by the Frank Silvera
Writer's Workshop at Urban Arts Corps.)

No Left Turn, 1978—Suavae Mitchell, Richard Gant, J.W. Smith, Duhart, B. T. Taylor, Bob Delbert, Doug Handy, Elwoodson Williams. (Written by Buriel Clay II. Directed by Richard Gant. Produced by the Frank Silvera Writer's Workshop at the Theatre of the Open Eye.)

Anna Lucasta, 1978—Debbie Allen. (Written by Philip Yordan. Directed by Ernestine M. Johnston. Produced by the New Federal Theatre at the Pilgrim Theatre, New York.)

Above: *Eubie!*, 1978—(Front row:) Lonnie McNeil, Jeffrey V. Thompson, Maurice Hines, Mel Johnson, Jr., Gregory Hines. (Conceived and directed by Julianne Boyd. Music by Eubie Blake. Choreography by Henry LeTang and Billy Wilson. Produced by Ashton Springer in association with Frank C. Pierson and Jay J. Cohen at the Ambassador Theater, New York.)

Below: *Eubie!*, 1979—Eubie Blake and members of the cast of *Eubie!* celebrate his 96th Birthday on stage.

The Daughters of the Mock, 1979—Barbara Montgomery, Frances Foster, Olivia Williams. (Written by Judi Ann Mason. Directed by Glenda Dickerson. Produced by the Negro Ensemble Company at the St. Marks Playhouse, New York.)

Coriolanus, 1979—Gloria Foster, Morgan Freeman. (Written by William Shakespeare. Directed by Michael Langham. Produced by Joseph Papp's New York Shakespeare Festival at the Anspacher Theater, New York.)

Benefit for the Frank Silvera Writer's Workshop, 1979—Geoffrey Holder and Carmen deLavalade re-create the dance they did with the *Josephine Baker Revue* in Paris in 1964, with the original costumes and orchestration.

Julius Caeser, 1979—Earle Hyman, Roscoe Orman, Robert Christian, Sonny Jim Gaines, Morgan Freeman, Clark Morgan, Gylan Kain, Count Stovall. (Written by William Shakespeare. Directed by Michael Langham. Produced by Joseph Papp's New York Shakespeare Festival at the Anspacher Theater, New York.)

Above: *Remembrance*, 1979—Roscoe Lee Brown, Earle Hyman. (Written by Derek Walcott. Directed by Charles Turner. Produced by Joseph Papp's New York Shakespeare Festival Workshop at Other Stage, New York.)

Below: *Inacent Black and the Five Brothers*, 1979—Valerie Drummond, Elaine Graham. (Written by A. Marcus Hemphill. Directed by Mikell Pinkney. Produced by the Billie Holiday Theatre; presented at the Black Theatre Festival/U.S.A. at Lincoln Center, New York.)

A Raisin in the Sun, 1979—Starletta Du Pois, Glynn Turman, Elizabeth Van Dyke. (Written by Lorraine Hansberry. Directed by Ernie McClintock. Produced by Woodie King, Jr. at the New Federal Theatre, New York.)

Above: *Amen Corner*, 1979—Ensemble cast. (Written by James Baldwin. Directed by Mical Whitaker. Produced by Kuumba Workshop of Chicago; presented at the Black Theatre Festival/ U.S.A. at Lincoln Center, New York.)

Below: *Daddy Goodness*, 1979—Clifton Davis, Carol-Jean Lewis. (Book by Shauneille Perry and Ron Miller. Based on the play of same title by Richard Wright and Louis Sapin. Lyrics by Ron Miller. Music by Ken Hirsch. Directed by Israel Hicks. Choreography and musical staging by Louis Johnson. Produced by Ashton Springer/Motown in association with Marty Markinson, Joseph Harris and Donald Tick at the Forest Theatre, PA.)

Zora Whu, 1979—Yvonne Taylor Cheyne, Yvonne Southerland, Laurence Holder. (Written by Laurence Holder. Directed by Yvonne Taylor Cheyne. Music by Jerry S. Jemmott. Produced by the 13th Street Theatre and YTC Repertory Theatre at the 13th Street Theatre, New York.)

Above: *One Mo' Time*, 1979—Sylvia "Kuumba" Williams, Thais Clark, Topsy Chapman, Vernel Bageneris. (Conceived and directed by Vernel Bageneris. Additional staging by Dean Irby. Musical arrangements by Lars Edegran and Orange Kellin. Special guest artist Dick Vance. Production consulting by Pepsi Bethel. Produced by Art D'Lugoff, Burt D'Lugoff, and Jerry Wexler in association with Shari Upbin at the Village Gate Downstairs Theatre, New York.)

Below: *Zooman and the Sign*, 1980—Giancarlo Esposito, Ray Aranha, Carl Gordon, Mary Alice. (Written By Charles Fuller. Directed by Douglas Turner Ward. Produced by the Negro Ensemble Company at Theatre Four, New York.)

An Evening with Josephine Baker, 1980—Marie Thomas, Joe Stanton. (Written by George Adams. Directed by Ernestine M. Johnston. Produced by Frank Silvera Writer's Workshop at The Leonard Davis Center, CCNY, New York.)

Above: *Season's Reason's*, 1980—Victor Willis, Smoky Stevens, Leon Thomas, Vonetta McGee, Ted Ross, Glynn Turman, Lou Fredricks. (Written by Ron Milner. Music by Charles Mason. Directed by Cliff Roquemore. Presented by the National Black Touring Circuit [Woodie King, Jr., Producer].)

Below: *boogie woogie landscape*, 1980—Marjorie Barnes, Calvin Lockhart. (Written by Ntozake Shange. Directed by Avery Brooks. Presented by the National Black Touring Circuit [Woodie King, Jr., Producer] at the Terrace Theatre, Washington, D.C.)

Not, 1981—Samuel L. Jackson, Catherine Slade, Bill Cobbs. (Written by Dan Owens. Directed by Dean Irby. Produced by the Frederick Douglass Creative Arts Center at the Lion Theatre, New York.)

Widows, 1981—Victoria Howard, Tina Sattin, Pamela Poitier. (Written by Mfundi Vundla. Directed by Vantile E. Whitfield. Produced by the New Federal Theatre at the Henry Street Settlement, New York.)

Zora, 1981—Phylicia Ayers-Allen. (A one-act play presented with *When the Chickens Came Home to Roost*. Written by Laurence Holder. Directed by Elizabeth Van Dyke. Produced by Woodie King, Jr. and Steve Tennen at the New Federal Theatre, New York.)

Left: *Long Day's Journey into Night*, 1981—Earle Hyman, Peter Francis-James, Gloria Foster, Al Freeman, Jr. (Written by Eugene O'Neill. Directed by Geraldine Fitzgerald. Produced by The Richard Allen Center for Culture and Art at St. Peter's Church, New York; later presented at The Public Theatre, New York.)

Above: *When Chickens Come Home to Roost*, 1981—Kirk Kirksey, Denzel Washington. (A one-act play presented with *Zora*. Written by Laurence Holder. Directed by Allie Woods. Produced by Woodie King, Jr. and Steve Tennen at the New Federal Theatre, New York.)

Keyboard, 1982—Cleavon Little, Lex Monson. (Written by Matt Robinson. Directed by Shauneille Perry. Produced by Woodie King, Jr., and Steve Tennen at the the New Federal Theatre, New York.)

Love to All Lorraine, 1982—Elizabeth Van Dyke. (Adapted by Elizabeth Van Dyke from the writings of Lorraine Hansberry. Presented by The National Black Touring Circuit [Woodie King, Jr., Producer].)

A Soldier's Play, 1981—Stephen Zettler, Cotter Smith, Adolph Caesar. (Written by Charles Fuller. Directed by Douglas Turner Ward. Produced by the Negro Ensemble Company at The Theatre Four, New York. Winner of the 1982 Pulitzer Prize for Best Play.)

A Soldier's Play, 1982—Brent Jennings, Steven A. Jones, Eugene Lee, Denzel Washington, Samuel L. Jackson, James Pickens Jr., Peter Friedman.

Tut-ankh-amen, The Boy King, 1982—Brel Barbara Clarke, Emil Herrera, Dianne Kirksey. (Written by Garland Lee Thompson. Directed by Chuck Wise. Produced by the Frank Silvera Writer's Workshop, New York.)

Ma Rainey's Black Bottom, 1984—(Left to Right:) Scott Davenport-Richards, Charles S. Dutton, Leonard Jackson, Theresa Merritt, Robert Judd, Joe Seneca; (Above:) Lou Criscuolo, John Carpenter. (Written by August Wilson. Directed by Lloyd Richards. Produced by the Yale Repertory Theater in association with Ivan Bloch, Robert Cole, and Frederick M. Zollo at the Cort Theater, New York.)

Some Playwrights,
Directors, Producers,
and Other Important People

The producers of *Bubbling Brown Sugar* (1976)—
Robert M. Cooper, Ashton Springer, Rosetta LeNoire
[concept], Richard Bell, J. Lloyd Grant.

Backstage at *Ceremonies in Dark Old Men* (1969)—
(Back row:) Denise Nicholas, Carl Lee, Gertha
Brock [costumes], Robert Freeman [rear],
unidentified, Billy Dee Williams, Bette
Howard, Arnold Johnson; (Front row:) Nate
Barnett, Richard Ward, Edmund Cambridge.

Opening Night of *Behold! Cometh the Vanderkellans*—
Harold Scott, Rosalind Cash, Roxie Roker, Woodie
King, Jr., [Producer], Diana Sands, Graham Brown,
Robert Christian.

Sam Barton (1985)—Director

Ernest Baxter—Lighting Designer

James Baldwin (1979)—Playwright

Townsend Brewster (1972)—Playwright

Hazel Bryant (1981)—Producer, Executive Director
of the Richard Allen Center for Culture and Art

Ed Bullins—Playwright

Edmund Cambridge (Circa 1979)—Production
Stage Manager, Director, Actor

Steve Carter (1978)—Playwright

Yvonne Taylor Cheyne (1979)—Director

Alice Childress (1970)—Playwright

Myrna Colley-Lee (1980)—Costume Designer

Walter Dallas (1983)—Director

Ossie Davis and Ruby Dee (1979)—Actors

Clifton Davis (1978)—Director

Leon B. Denmark—General Manager of the Negro
Ensemble Company

Judy Dearing—Costume Designer, Dancer, Actress

Owen Dodson (1980)—Playwright

Lonne Elder III (1973)   Playwright

Charles Fuller (1981)—Playwright

George Faison—Director, Choreographer

Roger Furman (1982)—Director, Founder and
Executive Director of the New Heritage Theatre

Irene Gandy (1984)—Press Agent

Paul Carter Harrison (1982)—Playwright

Fred Hudson (1981)—Executive Director of
the Frederick Douglass Creative Arts Center

A. Marcus Hemphill (1979)—Playwright

Linda Herring (1984)—Producer

Laurence Holder (1980)—Playwright

Dean Irby (1979)—Actor, Director

Stephanie Hughley (1980)—General
Manager, Producer

Langston Hughes, Vinnette Carroll, and
Ralph Bunch (1965)

The Founders of the Negro Ensemble Company—
Robert Hooks, Douglas Turner Ward, Gerald Krone.

C. Bernard Jackson—Executive Director
of Inner City Cultural Center, Los Angeles

Louis Johnson—Choreographer

Woodie King, Jr. (1973)—Producer Writer, Actor, Director

Duane L. Jones (1983) Actor, Director

Leslie Lee (1975)—Playwright

Clifford Mason—Playwright, Critic, Actor;
and Robert MacBeth— Director

Rosetta LeNoire (1980)—Executive Director
of AMAS Repertory, Actress, Producer

Ernie McClintock—Director and Founder
of 127th Street Repertory Ensemble

Arthur Mitchell—Founder and Executive
Director of Dance Theatre of Harlem

Loften Mitchell—Writer

John Oliver Killens (1979)—Writer

Dan Owens (1981)—Director

Coleridge-Taylor Perkinson (1979)—Composer

Shirley Prendergast (1982)—Lighting Designer

Shauneille Perry—Director, Actress, Writer, and Philip Hayes Dean—Playwright

Shirley Radcliffe—Executive Director of the
Richard Allen Center for Culture and Art

Vivian Robinson—Executive Director
of AUDELCO (Audience Development
Company)

Lloyd Richards (1979)—Director

Oz Scott—Director

Voza Rivers—Executive Director of the Roger Furman Theatre (formerly New Heritage Theatre); and Andre Robinson—Artistic Director of the Roger Furman Theatre

Michael Schultz (1968)—Director

Ntozake Shange (1979)—Playwright

Ted Shine (1970)—Playwright

Ashton Springer (1980)—Producer

Barbara Ann Teer (1980)—Executive Director of the
National Black Theatre

Garland Lee Thompson (1978)—Playwright, Artistic Director of
Frank Silvera Writer's Workshop

Horacena J. Taylor (1979)—Director

Melvin Van Peebles (1976)—Actor, Director,
Playwright, Filmmaker

Lisa T. Watson (1984)—Production Stage Manager

Sylvester N. Weaver, Jr. (1984)—Lighting Designer

Richard Wesley—Playwright

Samm-Art Williams (1979)—Playwright, Actor

(Top to Bottom:) Marshall Williams, Lighting Designer; Bernard Johnson,
 Costume Designer, Director, Dancer, Choreographer; Edward
Burbridge, Set Designer (Circa 1966)

BERT ANDREWS
In Conversation with
Paul Carter Harrison

HARLEM. BROADWAY. UPTOWN. DOWNTOWN. Two worlds apart where entertainment was concerned. I was born in Chicago, but I was raised in Harlem, where I got the bug to be part of the entertainment world at an early age. I went to interracial schools in New York and spent a lot of time going to movies. In fact, I saw so many movies that I thought I was white like everybody else on the screen until I became a teenager. I can remember playing hookey from school and going downtown to the Paramount Theatre to see Dean Martin and Jerry Lewis. When we came out of the theatre—two boys and two girls—we went to Child's Restaurant. We sat there for almost an hour and a half before we became aware that we were being ignored. Nobody spoke to us. And nobody served us. You know, nobody told us, "Nigger get out." Just nobody told us anything. Nobody spoke to us. Nobody served us. Finally, one of us went up to the headwaiter who informed us that Child's did not serve "colored" people. Till this very day I will not go into a Child's Restaurant.

I didn't know much about live theatre in those days, but I definitely wanted to be in show business as a singer or dancer. I was brought up around music. My mother was a music teacher, a church organist, and the national organist of the Independent Benevolent and Protective Order of Elks, so music was a constant in my life. It was no accident that I was drawn to this kind of life.

In the forties, Harlem was a different place. It was the period before integration, so we had our own clubs and bars uptown. And every bar had a piano, someplace where you could go sing. You could also pick up a few dollars singing in the after-hour clubs. One of my mentors was the pianist Billy Taylor, who was then playing over at a club called Wells. I used to go to Wells and sing every night. Billy took me under his wing, gave me a lot of advice, and kept me out of trouble. Once Billy even helped me write an act for the Club Baron. It was supposed to be an African extravaganza. The show was composed of two chorus lines. One had old, formerly retired chorus girls, and the other, guys in drag. Drag queens. I'd write a line, Billy would write a line. But by the time I had finished putting the project together, it was clear that Billy had done most of the writing.

I even had a manager in those days, a man named Al Andersen. He was wonderful to me. He was like a brother, a father. He put me on the audition circuit. I won the Apollo Amateur Night twice, but I never got my week to perform at the theatre. You see, I was young and impressionable then, and in those days, it was the sound of Billy Eckstine and Jimmy Rushing that was happening. The heavy blues and ballad singers. For example, I once did a recording for the army. Dick Hyman, a pianist who later became an important interpreter of diverse styles of jazz keyboard music, heard me sing. He liked my voice and called me in for the gig. The tune was called "V.D. Blues." The army was trying to hip GIs to venereal disease. During the recording session, the producers in the control room kept telling me to dirty-up my voice. They said my voice was too clean. I was too naive to understand what they were talking about, but the insinuation drove Dick crazy. Nobody wanted to simply say: "Listen man, you don't sound 'colored' "—that a more recognizable black voice was needed because they were targeting the recording to the black soldiers, as if it were only black troops that had a V.D. problem overseas. So the recording session was a disaster. They wanted to hear gut-bucket and I wanted to croon like Mel Torme or Nat Cole, even Johnny Mathis. Ironically, the way I kept my singing interests going was by joining the State Guard.

When the 369th National Guard was called up for service in Korea, the 15th Regiment State Guard was formed. I joined up so I could become part of the band and have an excuse to be out at night. I was still in high school, so the only excuse my mother would accept for my late night hours was band rehearsal. I'd get out in the street and hit Smalls Paradise, Wells, the Baby Grand, all the joints, including Joe Louis's club. Uptown was happening. Theatres like the Strand, and the Paramount had big band jazz, though the jazz scene of Fifty-Second Street was the main thing happening downtown. But there was *plenty* of great jazz uptown at the Hollywood, which featured an old upright piano, at Count Basie's Club, at the Heatwave, and certainly at Minton's Playhouse, the home of Be-bop music. In high school, we informally organized a band that would play at different social club affairs or after-school dances. Whoever got the gig would be the leader of the band for that particular occasion, since the leader got paid double. During this time, my first contact with the theatre was at the Harlem YWCA, where I auditioned for a role in *The Man Who Came to Dinner*. I was given this long, rambling speech. I was so bad, they laughed me out of the place. Clearly, I was not supposed to be in front of the camera.

I picked up photography in the army, but it was never just a hobby for me. It was more like a little hustle. When I was in Germany, GIs wanted to have pictures taken to send back home to their folks. After a while, the guys would seek me out to take the pictures, and I got pretty good at it. Plus, it was a way of picking up some extra change. It was fun, but it also became a sort of moonlighting gig for me which held my interest while I was serving Uncle Sam.

My regular job in the army—which was segregated at the time, despite an order from President Truman to desegregate in 1948— was creating on-duty education facilities for what was then called "Colored GIs." There were no similar facilities for the white GIs, and the white companies actually complained about "reverse discrimination." As I came out of the army, the schools were finally being integrated.

I was with the 7744 Educational Training Unit. My job was to establish these facilities throughout Europe. Within six weeks, the army was able to train us, as only the army can, giving us the teaching skills that usually required four years of college. But it wasn't easy. Here I am, a twenty-year-old big shot sergeant in the army with guys in my classes who are over thirty. These men were drafted into the army and I was supposed to motivate them to learn how to read and write. Part of the motivation was to tell them that learning to read and write was going to help them when they got back to civilian life. Then some guy from Alabama would raise his hand and say, "Teacher, I got four novelty stores back home, two Cadillacs, and my whole family working for me. What have you got?" I tell you, it was tough trying to teach some of those soldiers.

When I came out of the army, I went back to college briefly, and it was a moment that would pay off in the future. One of my school buddies was Bruce Llewellyn, who became the head of the New York office of the Small Business Administration. When I set up my photography business in 1966, he helped take the glitches out of the bureaucratic process. Anyway, my first job coming out of the army was with Lever Brothers, who had built this modern green glass building on Park Avenue. It was the first of the glass towers on Park Avenue, so it was a big deal that attracted many tourists. Having had a couple years of college, I was able to get this job in market research, which was a brand new field at that time. I later found out market research for us on the third floor was a euphemism for counting coupons. The market research area was also the favorite place to show off to the tourists. It was called "Little U.N." because we had a couple of Asians, a couple of African Americans, some whites, a few Latinos, and the tourists were impressed.

During this period, I was still dabbling in photography when I ran into Vernon Smith, a black photographer who I had admired for his ability to work as a professional. He told me that there was a black photographer on Fiftieth Street and Park Avenue, down the street from Lever Brothers, that I should meet. A black photographer on Park Avenue sounded exciting to me, so I arranged a meeting with the guy who turned out to be Chuck Stewart. He couldn't afford to hire an assistant at the time, but half-jokingly suggested that if I ever got fired and was collecting unemployment, he would subsidize an apprenticeship. So, I went back to Lever Brothers and quit my job, then returned to Chuck and said, "Hey man, guess what, I'm available!" When I told my mother, who was a woman with an unwavering Protestant work ethic, that I had quit my job so I could learn how to be a photographer, she exclaimed, "Fool! That's what white people do for a hobby!" And she was right, too.

At least that's how it appeared to me during the fifties. I went to work for Chuck, who subsidized my unemployment check with twenty-five dollars per week. He would take me out to lunch, sometimes dinner. I even slept at the studio at times. For three years, I did everything from run errands, develop and process film, carry his bags—whatever had to be done, even babysit for his kids. So it was an apprenticeship in the classic sense of the word. He would give me assignments like, "Go shoot sunlight!" And I'd ask, "Shoot sunlight . . .? How do you shoot air?" Then I'd go out and really work at it. Chuck was not only my mentor. He became a friend, even a father figure, though we were close in age. We had a ball.

I probably would have become a jazz photographer if Chuck were not already into jazz. The theatre later became propitious because I needed another subject matter that would not have me competing with my mentor. Sports photography or simply portrait photography never interested me, so whatever the new theme, it would have to be in the performing arts. It could've turned out to be dance because I was shooting a lot of dancers involved with jazz music. Another reason for finding my own thing was a feeling that my work was beginning to look too much like Chuck's —not unusual with an assistant. But, one of the things that Chuck taught me was that there are no secrets. Not really. Somebody may come up with a new technique, but then anyone else can use it. What's unique is the photographer's eye—you can't borrow someone else's perspective. When Chuck thought I knew enough about being a professional, he "fired" me—gave me a camera and a roll of film and said, "All right, buddy, you're on your own."

I later went to work for Charlie Banks, who had started a magazine called *Social Whirl*. It came out every week, and I was the sole photographer. I was living at an SRO hotel in the West Nineties where I shared a bathroom and a kitchen with three students from Columbia University. At night, when it was dark, I'd put a blanket up to my window and put some trays on the table and print. And during the day, I'd wash them in the common bathroom. I kept a little Federal enlarger in a suitcase which I would set up on the bureau, and I turned out good stuff for the magazine.

Unfortunately, those prints went up in the fire in my studio in 1985. You see, those prints, which dealt with popular black life around town, would have been very valuable now because they represented the social life of a segregated city. We still couldn't do much downtown, so every week *Social Whirl* would announce where the fashion shows, dances, and parties were happening. The social events at the Theresa Hotel, the balls at the Renaissance Ballroom, the bands at the Savoy. We covered the whole community. We even covered a story of blacks in the Fire Department and won the first Vulcan Award, presented to us by the Vulcan Society, an organization created by the black firefighters in New York. It was winter, and they had me out there chasing fire trucks. But the thing that really made the magazine was the fact that the style-conscious ladies of Harlem did not shop at Bloomingdale's or Saks Fifth Avenue. They had their own couturiers. Fashion was prominent uptown. I've gotta say that the best-dressed women in New York City, probably in the world, were in Harlem at that point in time. A party or event would be coming up, and a personal dressmaker would make a Chanel or Balenciaga number for the ladies overnight. So I got to shoot a lot of fashion during that time.

Of course, I still made the club circuit as well as the entertainment palaces like the Apollo. I even got to shoot many of the comedians, like Pigmeat Markham and George Wiltshire. Those guys were post-minstrel performers, vaudevillians. In fact, George was a great friend. I spent a lot of time at the Apollo, where Willie Bryant was the emcee. I got a great picture of him before he died. Willie was a very popular man in Harlem, though hardly known downtown, despite the fact that he was one of the first black comedians from Harlem to have an opportunity to perform on Broadway—with Ethel Waters and Jose Ferrer during the Forties in *Mamba's Daughters*. Other great acts that played mostly Harlem included Butter Beans and Suzy, Moms Mabley, and Nipsy Russell, who was one of the first to break away from the impression that all black humor was too "blue" for popular consumption, too dirty. Particularly on television. Too "blue" was the excuse given to keep blacks out of television even after they cleaned up their acts. And a similar charge was launched against the early beginnings of the Black Theatre movement, which often used the kind of four-letter words that are now common throughout global entertainment. Still, Pigmeat Markham, in my estimation, will always be the quintessential vaudevillian. A classic skit would be Pigmeat coming across the stage with a case of beer and the straight man asking, "Where you goin', man?"—to which Pigmeat replies, "I'm taking my case to court!" Later he shows up with a ladder and tells the straight man, "I'm takin' my case to a higher court!" A lot of white comedians, such as Abbott and Costello, have borrowed much from Pigmeat and others uptown.

133

Anyway, I was making a living as a photographer. And part of making that living was taking pictures for the *Amsterdam News*. You got five dollars for the first one and three dollars for the second, and fifteen if your picture turned up on the front page. My first fifteen-dollar photo was of a guy who went crazy in the subway and I got a shot of two cops bringing him up the stairs. I just happened to be standing there when they struggled up the stairs with him. I wasn't on any crusade or anything, so the moment didn't seem too unusual. I was just gigging. So there was nothing overly significant about the shot other than it got the front page of the *Amsterdam News*. But that was an entirely different world. My world was *Our World* and *Sepia* magazine. I was trying to make a living doing weddings, babies, bar mitzvahs, and have a good time doing it. Nothing heavy about it.

In fact, the aesthetics of photography didn't come for me until much, much, later. Guys like Chuck Stewart got started in photography in high school. They got their first cameras for graduation presents. At age twenty-four or twenty-five I got into photography late and was always in a hurry to catch up. I was pursuing show business, having a good time. I didn't get to work on my first black theatre production until 1959: a Harlem production of *Dark of the Moon* directed by Vinnette Carroll, and starring Cicely Tyson.

My entree to the production was Cicely, whom I had met casually crossing Eighth Street in the Village. It was during the time I was working and taking pictures for Ophelia Devore, which was the first really successful black model agency. Cicely was one of her models—as were, at one time or another, Diahann Carroll, Lucille Rich, Sue Simmons, Hal DeWindt, and Gil Noble. I had recognized Cicely from a cover photo Chuck Stewart had made of her with Hal DeWindt for *Our World* magazine. We got into a conversation. She liked what I was about and what she was doing sounded exciting. So we started dating. Cicely asked Vinnette if I could come to the Harlem YWCA to shoot the production, and Vinnette said fine. I was grateful to be allowed to come, and was a little terrified because it was my first time photographing theatre, and also because Vinnette could be very imposing. That production also had Roscoe Lee Browne, Clarence Williams III, Louise Stubbs, Pawnee Sills, Dick Ward, and Leah Scott. The stage manager was Ellis Hazelip. There I was with this incredible collection of talented people all of whom would become major personalities in the theatre during the following decades. That was my first taste of working in the theatre and I just fell in love with it. I began to think about theatre and to become familiar with a few black workshops. I soon discovered that a black theatre world actually existed both in Harlem and in Greenwich Village, away from Broadway. Then Jean Genet's *The Blacks* was produced off-Broadway in 1961 and really opened my eyes.

Almost every major black actor of the period performed in *The Blacks* at one time or another. The original cast had Roscoe Lee Browne, James Earl Jones,

Cynthia Belgrave, Louis Gossett, Jr., Ethel Ayler, Helen Martin, Cicely Tyson, Godfrey Cambridge, Lex Monson, Raymond St. Jacques, Jay J. Riley, Maya Angelou, Charles Gordon, and Charles Campbell. Included among the luminaries that played in subsequent productions are Thelma Oliver, Lincoln Kirkpatrick, Vinnie Burrows, Harold Scott, Robert Hooks, Moses Gunn, Louise Stubbs, Max Glanville, Clebert Ford, and Billy Dee Williams. I was always impressed with Louis Gossett, Jr., whom I thought of as an astute actor. Lou used *The Blacks* for his personal workshop. Every time a male actor would leave a role, Lou would shift over into that part and study it. Unfortunately, I didn't get to photograph the original cast. Martha Swope, whose work is widely represented on Broadway, shot that. Max Eisen, the press agent for the show, gave me a shot at the replacement call, and has used me ever since—including hiring me for my first Broadway play, *The Subject Was Roses*, which won a Pulitzer Prize.

Cicely was the one who first introduced me to black theatre. She was always easy for me to work with because she had a good sense of self. For example, Cicely has always been very careful about what parts she would take, and I have seen her turn down parts that she felt were not right, not good for her. She may have needed the job, but if she felt that the part was either demeaning or not right for her, she would turn it down. Cicely was the one who encouraged me to do head shots of actors—a natural outgrowth of my involvement in the theatre. By that time, my love affair with the theatre allowed me to become very excited about the talent that surrounded me. Nobody had much money in those days, so I often worked with actors on a promise that I would be compensated in the future, simply because I enjoyed working with them. I met Robert Guilliame—who now has his own T.V. sitcom—when he was doing *Purlie Victorious* on Broadway. He was a fabulous talent, and I tried to encourage him to come to the studio for a photo session. Two years later, when he was moving out to the West Coast, he called and hired me to do his portraits. I once did photos for Altovise Gore when she appeared in an Equity Library Theatre production of *Blithe Spirits*. She needed the photos urgently, but before she could pay for them, she was cast in the road company of *Golden Boy* with Sammy Davis, Jr.—who she subsequently married. I didn't hear from her for a long time. And just when things were getting financially rough, I opened the mailbox, and there it was, a check from Altovise which paid my rent for a month.

The late Godfrey Cambridge was another great personality on the rise who often recommended me to various projects. Unfortunately, the only shots I have of Godfrey and his wife Barbara Ann Teer are photos which I had given them as a wedding gift. I loved Godfrey. He was a strange, troubled man. He had a serious sleeping problem, too. Godfrey would call his friends in the wee hours of the morning. I was a night person because I worked all night. Godfrey would call me at two o'clock in the morning and talk for an hour. He was moving into the entertainment mainstream and would always hear about work projects. For example, when RCA first produced its color television, the current technology of color bars was not yet used to determine color balance. The balance was based upon skin tones. They discovered that Godfrey, because of his dark complexion, had the perfect skin tone to achieve color balance for the tube. RCA decided to run ads in *Life Magazine* about their new color tubes. They had planned to send Godfrey to a white photographer, but he refused to do the ad unless they used me. In addition, they would have to pay me on the same scale they would've paid the white photographer. It was not unusual in those days—or these—for a black photographer to be paid less than his white counterpart. RCA was furious, but Godfrey had the perfect skin tone so they had to live with his demands. We made big, beautiful, tight color shots of Godfrey's smiling face, advertising his skin tone as the perfect color balance for RCA television sets. They ran those ads all over the place.

Pulitzer Prize-winning playwright Chuck Gordone is another actor who personally helped give my career a huge boost. Chuck was directing a version of *Detective Story* for the Equity Library Theater. Godfrey Cambridge was in that production as well. Chuck asked me to do a free photo session with the cast so that he could have a personal record of the production. He later helped me sell the photos to the actors. Patrick and Joy McGinnis—a husband and wife team who were directors of the ELT—liked what I had done and invited me to shoot other productions for them. I didn't get paid for the productions, but they worked out a plan that gave me complete access to the actors. ELT was my first regular institutional gig. Then the direction of ELT was taken over by Lyle Dye, Jr., followed by Fred Williams, David Marlin Jones, and Shepard Traub. I stayed on. Dick Moore, a press agent for Equity who was revamping a magazine for Actor's Equity, took a special interest in me and greatly influenced the direction in which I was headed. Dick hired me to shoot the Equity meetings for the new union house organ. So now I began to move intimately in the world of theatre.

Active involvement in the theatre was not always encouraged in the early sixties. I had a pretty fair little reputation off-Broadway. I was doing a lot of hustling so I became fairly well known. I'd go see the producers. I'd go see the press agents. I'd go see whomever would look at my portfolio and possibly give me a job. If I knew somebody who was directing a play, I'd call him and ask if he'd introduce me to the press agent. If I knew an actor, I'd ask the actor to recommend my portfolio to the director. I once took time to shoot a picture of a "gofer"—the guy running errands on a show, as in "gofer lunch, gofer coffee" —and his girlfriend, because today's gofer is tomorrow's producer. Sure enough, a couple of years later, the gofer became a producer and hired me for a show. My first "real" Equity production was *2 By Sarayon* in 1961. While sitting in Downey's with my friend Barrie Novak, a friend of hers named Arthur Storch came in and asked us to have a drink with him to celebrate his just having signed a contract to direct his first off-Broadway production. In one of the lead roles was young Alvin Ailey. Barrie and I both jumped on him, "Who's your photographer?" He told me to call him and bring my portfolio, which I did. He then introduced me to the producers as his choice of photographer—I got the job!

I made rounds just like all the actors did. I took my portfolio to one press agent who examined my shots of *Dark of the Moon* and a few ELT productions and said, "Gee, you've got some nice stuff here but I don't have any colored shows this year." That same press agent hired me many times in later years.

In fact, as I go through my old copies of *Theatre World*, an annual book which lists all the productions of the previous year, it turns out that over the long run, I finally ended up doing more white shows than black shows. I've been listed as one of the contributing photographers in *Theatre World* now for twenty years. When my studio went up in smoke, I called John Willis, of *Theatre World*, and told him that I was trying to reconstitute my files. Less than ten days later I got two big packages on my doorstep with a complete file of every *Theatre World*.

I came along in an era when off-Broadway was an important, viable, vibrant, rich, busy place. And there were plays and openings every day, every night. There were so many plays and openings—that an organization called the League of Theaters was formed to discourage three or four plays from opening on the same night, each competing for the important critical reviewers. It was a time when a play might go into production for as little as ten-thousand dollars. And most of the openings were black-tie events. Theatre was fun. And there was plenty of work. I was not making a lot of money because nobody off-Broadway could earn too much on a show that was produced for ten-thousand dollars. But I was doing all right. I was paying my rent. Just like Sean Walker said of me in a recent interview at the Schomburg, "Now here's a guy that has been doing his thing. Now he ain't rich!. . . Never made a whole bunch of money. But he has had a good time doing what he does."

I was busy. But there was a lot of work I didn't get to do because it was restricted—more, perhaps, by the competition than by race. I would have loved to have shot Chuck Gordone's Pulitzer Prize-winning play, *No Place to Be Somebody*, but Friedman and Abels who habitually did Broadway—as did Van Dam Studios before them—got the job. They also shot Sammy Davis, Jr.'s production of *Golden Boy*. So while I did a tremendous amount of off-Broadway work, I seldom got to Broadway. It's political. That's how it works in this business. When Friedman and Abels finally decided that they would retire, my reputation off-Broadway was strong enough for me to believe that I would pick up a good share of the business. However, Dorothy Ross, a major Broadway press agent who was a friend, employer and mentor to me, felt that it would be difficult at that time for a black photographer to get much work on Broadway. I didn't believe her at first because I was doing so well off-Broadway. I was

137

convinced that as the people I worked with went to Broadway, they would take me with them. With the exception of good friends like Dorothy Ross and Ashton Springer, it didn't happen. It might've started out racially, but after a while it became political—I just didn't have the name and connections that others had.

I remember when the production of *Home* by the NEC moved to Broadway. The new producers, of course, brought in their own press agent. Gerald Krone, general manager of the NEC, insisted that he use me as photographer. The press agent went along reluctantly, but feeling pressured, he informed Jerry that the pictures I took during the photo call were absolutely unusable, and that he found it necessary to have another call with a different photographer. I was furious. Nonetheless, while the new photo call for *Home* was in progress, I quickly processed my prints and ran them around to *Newsweek* and *Time* and other people that I knew and sold quite a few—which certainly salvaged my ego! It wasn't the first time I had to come through the back door with my photos.

One of my earliest experiences as a professional photographer was working for *Sepia* magazine, which had tried to compete with *Ebony* magazine. *Sepia* was owned by a wealthy Texan, George Levitan. Nobody ever called him George. He was always referred to as Mister Levitan. His family owned miles and miles and miles of warehouses down in Fort Worth, Texas that they leased to the government and U.S. Rubber. Levitan was a flamboyant Texan, the kind of guy that wore diamonds in his boots. He hired me as part of a team to go across the country doing magazine stories. When we got down to Fort Worth, he kicked his legs up on the table and told us that he knew "colored people" very well because his favorite program was "Amos and Andy." And the man was dead serious. Now, the editor of his magazine was a local black woman. Levitan was very fond of telling us, and anybody who would listen, how he had found this woman in the cotton fields and had educated her and made her the editor of his magazine. He thought of it as a "colored" success story. He often bragged about the Cadillac he gave her each year. And it was true. Every year he would buy himself a brand new Cadillac and give her his old one.

Levitan was the Great White Father of all time. I was young and had not much experience. In fact, all I had was a Rolliflex camera and a flash—we didn't even have strobes then. Levitan wanted us to shoot the rodeo. But this was still Fort Worth, Texas, and despite his clout in town, black people could only go to the rodeo on Thursdays. He decided to give a banquet to show off his black professionals from New York. I didn't have much in the way of clothing, mostly t-shirts and khaki pants. And that had more to do with deprivation than style. So he took us down into town and bought us tuxedos. I needed real clothes, not a tuxedo! After the banquet, I wore the tuxedo all the way to California.

The trip to California was an eye-opener. We drove a rented station wagon cross-country in the chill of winter. The fact that black people could only go to the rodeo in Fort Worth once a week did not compare with my first direct and personal encounters with segregation. It was the pits. At one point, we got caught in a blizzard. We couldn't go through a pass in Amarillo, Texas that was blocked off by police. Traffic was not being allowed to pass because of the weather, and we were unable to find a hotel or motel to take us in for the night. The police told us we would have to find a private home somewhere that might be willing to put us up for the night. Throughout the trip, we had been purchasing sandwiches at various grocery stores and using the car as a restaurant. The car now became our motel. We slept in the cold. That was one miserable night. One of the things I discovered on that trip—having recently returned from my army stint in Europe, where I fell in love with the landscape— was that America was just as beautiful as Europe. It is a fabulous country. I loved the country, but hated the people in it.

In Los Angeles, we were staying downtown at the Ambassador Hotel. Here I am for the first time in Los Angeles and the first time alone, when I spot Huntington Hartford. I had remembered meeting him in New York while doing some freelance work for Dave Hepburn, who had been a speech writer for President Roosevelt and was editor for *Our World* magazine. Hartford had just built a new theatre, the Huntington Hartford Theatre. He was coming out of the theatre with a stunning black woman. The moment I saw them, I started taking some shots. Hartford approached me and asked if I was from *Ebony* or *Jet*. I told him I was with *Sepia*. He then announced that the lady in his company was his new star, Loray White, and allowed me to take several more shots of her in front of the theatre. Back at the hotel, the editor on the junket was annoyed that I had taken time away from my designated assignment to photograph Loray White, dismissing her as a nobody; he said I was wasting time with a pretty face. We forwarded the photos to Levitan, who rejected them for the same reasons as the editor. Soon after, he fired his three slick black professionals from New York because he thought we were just too slick. But the negatives were returned to me. I figured maybe I could use them someday. Less than six months later, following the debacle with Kim Novak, Sammy Davis, Jr. married Loray White. Now Levitan was only too happy to have the photos. I sold them all back to *Sepia*.

Working in this business is like an ongoing improvisation. Little twists of fate have also followed me into the theatre world. A guy stopped me casually on the street one day and my whole life changed. He told me about Larry Feldman, a producer packaging shows for Westport, Connecticut; Mineola, Long Island; and the Paper Mill Theatre in New Jersey. His star packages consisted of people like Jane Fonda, Myrna Loy, and Walter Pigeon, who would appear on the circuit for one or two weeks. My friend, who was a photographer, recommended me to Feldman because I was doing theatre. I went to see Feldman, who said that his press agent Larry Witchal did all the hiring, so whatever Larry said was okay with him. Witchal liked my portfolio and I started working for Feldman. He brought in just about every major Hollywood star of the time. I felt comfortable working on these star-packaging projects because I had begun to develop casual relationships with many of the actors who hung out at Jim Downey's restaurant, across the street from where I lived. I spent a lot of time at Downey's, and I built up a reputation among the actors, producers, and directors who hung out there as this up-and-coming, hot shot, young black photographer. Downey's was famous for the celebrity photos that covered the walls. The criteria for making the wall was an actor had to be currently working and also be a regular patron. Before long, Downey started sending me out to take pictures of working actors on Broadway, which gave me a different kind of access to actors. Ninety-nine percent of the actors were white, since that was the ratio working Broadway. But I did manage to get Ben Vereen placed on the wall, for *Jesus Christ Superstar*.

During this time, I had done a lot of work for Gerald Krone and Dorothy Olim, a husband and wife team of producers and managing directors. They liked my work, so when the Negro Ensemble Company was being formed by Gerald, Douglas Turner Ward, and Robert Hooks in 1967, I was asked to be the resident photographer. Both Doug and Bobby were familiar with my work because I had earlier photographed a production of Doug's two one-act plays *Days of Absence* and *Happy Ending*—which were produced by Bobby, and which subsequently led to the formation of the NEC. My first shoot with NEC was on their first show, *Song of the Lusitanian Bogey*. This show gave me a bit of trouble at first, because it was a non-linear, ritualistic play that changed quite a lot during rehearsals. There I was on the first day of rehearsals—with no costumes, no settings, no lights, not even a notion about the script. I couldn't tell how they were going to put this show together, or how I would be able to shoot suitable photos for the newspapers. Fortunately, Michael Shultz was a terrific director who knew what he was after, even if I didn't. It was his first major project and he was excited, but I was not sure how to shoot something that had not yet been formed. Michael sat down and explained the play and the ensemble concept to me, then directed me toward some interesting set-ups. He was not the kind of director who was concerned that the audience might reject the play if they didn't see the precise moment that had been captured for the photo in the Sunday *New York Times*.

While a photo does not always represent accurately what is happening in the play, it should at least illuminate the play's intentions. One of my favorite photos is of Cleavon Little in *The Ofay Watcher*. I was having a hard time finding the picture for the *New York Times* that, for me, best represented the play. I spent most of my picture call setting up a very difficult double exposure shot of Cleavon Little, naked from the waist up. On the right side of the photo are

Billie Allen and Terry Kiser, against a black background. The double exposure, the black background, and the black woman and white man off to the side gave the picture an ominous quality that was beautiful. The *Times* hated it! I think they hated it essentially because it was too much black. Not racially black, but too much black background. Newspapers hate pictures with lots of black background, because in printing they just eat up ink. And then they reproduce muddy—they're very difficult to reproduce. So whenever possible, the papers avoid pictures that have a lot of black in them. I think the picture was just too dark for them. But I love it. It is one of my favorite pictures.

Capturing the intention of a play requires different methods. The designed set-up is easiest because it gives me more latitude in terms of sets and costumes, as well as the advantage of using existing lights. Sometimes, particularly off-Broadway, auxiliary lighting is needed, thus I've gotten into the habit of always carrying along extra lights so that I don't lose the opportunity to get a good picture. There is also a time factor in photo calls. Usually, according to the union, you get two hours for a drama and three hours for a musical. It doesn't always work that way. Sometimes you get an hour; at times, only half an hour. Sometimes, on Broadway, a play is shot candid. The photographer is invited to a dress rehearsal to get shots while the play is in progress. You try to get a spontaneous effect in the image. Sometimes, a special dress run-through for the photographer is called, which results in semi-candid shots. During these sessions, the photographer has the authority to ask for a repetition of an action, or mood, or attitude. Generally, a photo call is orchestrated by the director or stage manager, who might have a list of specific scenes he or she feels are necessary to describe the intention of the play. I have done photo calls that required immediate improvisations or adjustments because of the state of readiness—or unreadiness—of the production, or the general disposition, for better or worse, of the performers. Once I had to shoot Phil Silvers and Sandy Dennis down in the lounge of the theatre because the stage was being painted. Sandy had on a large shawl. Phil spontaneously climbed under the shawl so that they both were wearing it. Pow! That was the shot. On another occasion, I had to shoot Al Pacino in his first play, *The Indian Wants the Bronx*, down at the Astor Place Theatre. It was snowing and the theatre was in a fit of production chaos—lumber all over the place, the stage occupied with technicians, simply no place to shoot the pictures. When I asked what the play was about and was told about a scene in a telephone booth, Howard Atlee, the press agent, and I herded Al and the cast out into the snow and into a nearby telephone booth on the corner. And that was the series of shots they used.

Working for some directors is not so easy. Everybody has their own sense of urgency. The press agent is concerned with getting photos out to the press on time; the director is concerned with completing a scene and couldn't care less about stopping for a photo call. And the photographer enters with his urgent concern for both precise technical response and for finding a moment of spontaneity. I remember taking photos of a run-through of Amiri Baraka's two one-acters—*The Toilet* and *The Slave*—down at the St. Marks Place Theatre the year before NEC took over the space. I sat down next to Amiri, and began shooting. It was close to opening and the atmosphere was tense. Everybody was on edge, fighting, fussing, and feuding, and this was the only time I could get pictures for the producer. The clicking of the camera lens was apparently too loud for Baraka, so he threw me out before I could complete the assignment. Fortunately, I had enough shots to meet the urgent needs of the press agent.

Sometimes the time pressure on the press agent is so great that he or she might send the leads of a play into my studio without even a glance at the script, let alone a single rehearsal. At this point, I am asked to invent something that makes sense, at least photographically, for the public. The image might have nothing to do with the play, but the press agent will insist on something that flatters the personality of the lead actor regardless of the role he has to play, so that posters can be made for advanced sales. There was a period down at the Henry Street Settlement when the New Federal Theatre was having a hard time getting pictures placed in the New York press. We had to shoot pictures in rehearsal rooms—which are usually bare rooms with no lights or scenery— against the brick walls of the building, thus all the pictures came out looking the same, irrespective of the play. I had to start inventing settings and costumes that might resemble what the plays were about. We corrected this by using large flats which were "borrowed" from current shows, and sometimes even shooting in front of the stage curtain—which then required very careful lighting to keep the subjects from "disappearing" into the black curtain. But sure enough, the photos began appearing in the papers again. Still, we had to take time away from the rehearsals, a half-hour here or there, for set-ups. Most directors are annoyed when they have to lose time to photo calls. There are some directors, however, like Douglas Turner Ward, who understand instinctively the impor- tance of the pictures. He's a dream director to work with on a photo call. It would be easy to suspect that Douglas worked so well because he originally came into the business as an actor, but the truth of the matter is that Douglas always knew we were recording history. He always seemed to have a sense of what the picture should be about in addition to understanding the text of the play. Then there is Jerry Krone, who is not a photographer nor otherwise a visual artist. Still, he taught me a great deal about the visual possibilities of theatre productions. Jerry would sit down with me, go through my contact sheets, and through re-cropping, reveal to me certain visual tensions that gave me pictures I had not seen. Jerry was a wonderful teacher. On one occasion, Jerry brought the cast to my studio to make photos for the NEC production of *Daughters of the Mock*. We didn't have costumes, so we draped the ladies in black cloth and shot their heads emerging from blackness. Lighting was critical against so much black background in order to assure that the print would be reproducible. Of all the photos taken that day, the particular shot that was the most successful, dramatically and commercially, had nothing to do with the play. That photo, with three strong and beautiful women—Frances Foster, Barbara Montgomery, and Roxie Roker—became my first poster.

By this time, I had begun to accept that I was a theatrical specialist, though I still had no sense of making history. I doubt if the actors in the company were able to project themselves into a historical framework either. What we all felt at NEC was a kind of collective participation in this unusual opportunity to work at our crafts, whether it was acting, set designing, or photography. I was happy to be a working professional in a very exciting environment. Those early years, and my subsequent years at NEC, spawned so many important personalities in theatre, film, and television—including Michael Schultz, Rosalind Cash, Roxie Roker, Esther Rolle, Moses Gunn, Phylicia Allen Rashaad, Frances Foster, Denzel Washington, Adolph Caesar, Charles Fuller, Barbara Montgomery, Hattie Winston, Giancarlo Esposito, to mention but a few. It was also the place where many black technicians, such as the stalwart Horacena Taylor, and Clinton Turner Davis, and others, developed skills that led them to directing.

Working so intimately with the NEC helped me to pay attention to the nuances of actors in the industry in general, so that I could appreciate the challenge of recognizing that certain spark that made my work more than a job. I'm talking about the sophisticated wit of a Josephine Premise or the intensity of the late Diana Sands. And the earthy power of Gloria Foster, whom I have loved since her first New York show, *In White America*. And then I think of the genius of the late Charlie Smalls, who wrote the score for *The Wiz*, the mercurial Melvin Van Peebles, and the bigger-than-life presence of Geoffrey Holder. Shooting any of these people requires a different point of view. Al Freeman, Jr., for example, is the kind of actor from whom you can always get a wonderful photograph. No matter what Al might be feeling inwardly or personally, you can always be assured, because of his professional commitment, that he will give you the appropriate attitude for the pictures. You have to work harder with some people than with others. There are some actors from whom you can get marvelous things if you can photograph them while they are acting and if they can lose themselves in a role. But the moment that you alert them to what you're doing, they step out of that role and you're in trouble. Then you've gotta make all kinds of adjustments.

Professional actors will usually trust my point of view. They trust me because first we have a consultation, we sit down and talk. They then decide during the consultation that they trust me, or that they'll take a chance. And I can tell from the consultations whether or not I'm going to have problems and what the problems are going to be. Unlike California actors—movie actors—stage actors have no idea what they look like when they sit in front of a camera.

143

They are as self-conscious as anybody else that must face a camera. Rip Torn came to me once to make some photos for commercials. He trusted me as a photographer because I had done some of his stage shows. But the pictures never worked because Rip couldn't see himself as a commercial person. I made some great photos for his theatre work. But he never really got into his commercial shots.

Many people had made the erroneous assumption that because I worked so intimately with the NEC, the most visible producing institution of black plays, I was working throughout the black theatre community. Many other groups were operating in New York at the time, but with the exception of the independent commercial productions, I was not asked by other institutions to photograph their shows. Institutions like the New Lafayette Theatre in Harlem, for example, didn't hire me to shoot their productions. At the National Black Theatre in Harlem, Barbara Ann Teer was basically busy with ritual theatre, and was not interested in commercial photos. I'm not sure why I was not called into Harlem to photograph the productions of Roger Furman's New Heritage Theatre or Ernie McClintock's Afro-American Studio Theatre. I suspect it had more to do with their focus, which was essentially community based, and it also had a little to do with their budgets. However, Garland Thompson invited me to be his official photographer and to record the workshop productions at the Frank Silvera Writer's Workshop, which was directed toward the development of professional writers. I also photographed productions for Hazel Bryant's Richard Allen Cultural Center, formerly known as the Afro-American Total Theatre, as well as for the Frederick Douglass Creative Arts Center, and the Billie Holiday Theatre in Brooklyn. One of the biggest hits that I've been involved with in Harlem was *Mama, I Want to Sing*.

Now here is a show without a mainstream theatre audience that has, as of this writing, been running for at least five years largely due to the ingenuity of its producer, Vi Higgins. I was one of the original photographers of *Mama, I Want to Sing* when it was presented at Fordham University at Lincoln Center in a small gospel showcase production that was mostly concertized with a loosely structured book. It later moved to Harlem where it was presented with a more formal presentation and good technical support. The survival of the show had nothing to do with Broadway or off-Broadway critical reviews. It was supported entirely by the Harlem community through word-of-mouth. There was very little publicity, at first. People went to see the production two, three, even four times before television commercials started to appear and give the play a whole new life. The Harlem audience was supplemented by black church groups that were bussed in by Vi Higgins from around the Metropolitan area. Vi had created an audience. The play had the same kind of community-based appeal and support that *Inascent Black* had in Brooklyn, where it played for two years at the Billie Holiday Theatre before Ashton Springer brought it to Broadway.

144

The original impulse to create an audience in Brooklyn and Harlem has allowed the Black Theatre to have a continuing presence away from the commercial manipulation of Broadway. Today, Black Theatre has become a cultural factor all over the country. Legitimate playhouses for black plays have sprung up in places as remote from Broadway as Phoenix, Minneapolis, Denver, Durham, Atlanta, just about everywhere black people are living. History will prove that while efforts were being made to create theatre in the shadow of the Great White Way, those efforts had nothing to do with "me and my shadow." In other words, the Black Theatre was not trying to copy a tradition as much as trying to create a tradition which, in style and content, had relevance as entertainment and social illumination for the black community.

Actually, it was Woodie King, Jr., director/producer of the New Federal Theatre, who made me aware that what I had been doing all along simply as a job had now become part of a history with archival significance. At a certain moment, it occurred to me that I didn't have any photos of Roger Furman, a man who had insulated himself in Harlem writing, producing and directing his plays. Also teaching. Doing very creditable work. An archive would be incomplete without him, so I arranged a meeting unaware of how ill he was. He was more than willing to spend an afternoon laughing and chatting while being photographed along Riverside Drive. I now have the last pictures of Roger Furman.

Fate being what it is, three weeks before the January 1985 fire that destroyed my files, I was trying to get a grant from a funding agency to buy fireproof files and was turned down. A few months earlier, I had begun to organize my files so that I could have a clearer picture of the broader context of the photos I had made over the past thirty years, photos that went as far back as the fifties in Harlem, like the opening day shots of a rib-joint opened by Sidney Poitier after doing one of his first films. Reviewing the photos gave me a sense of self-definition that I had not paid much attention to earlier. Unfortunately, I was not used to the world of grantsmanship, and was unable to save such a valuable collection with fireproof files. Grantsmanship was new to me.

I also, perhaps naively, anticipated receiving a grant to work on a documentary film on Austin Hansen, who in my estimation, was one of the most important black photographers ever, as the recent exhibit at the Schomburg Library certainly proves. Hansen was equal to, if not more important than James Van Der Zee, who was an extraordinary studio photographer during his time. But, while Van Der Zee's clients were mostly middle class people who came to his studio, Hansen was a photographer of the folk. He was more of a street photographer. He did the churches, the lodges, the sports figures, and the Harlem nightclub scene. I wanted very much to do a documentary on this man who missed out on fame because Van Der Zee was discovered first. Many of my contemporaries influenced my work—people like Chuck Stewart, of course;

Bob Green, who shoots many stills for motion picture productions; Tony Barboza, an art photographer who also broke into fashion and advertising; and Monetta Sleet, a photo journalist who produced a prodigious amount of work with *Ebony* magazine. Sleet's work, which includes everything from the civil rights era, to emerging African nations to vice in Harlem, was recently exhibited at the New York Public Library under the sponsorship of Phillip Morris. And people like Roy deCorava, whose classic book with text by Langston Hughes, *Sweet Flypaper of Life*, was recently reissued in a beautiful new edition and who actually found my first studio for me on 39th street, and bullied and cajoled me into "making the move downtown." And, of course, there is the renaissance man himself, Gordon Parks, a contemporary role model who received his initial recognition through his photojournalistic work with *Life* magazine in the late forties and fifties. The breadth of his work includes the authorship of books and screenplays, the direction of films, and the composition of symphonies and ballet scores. Gordon is truly a man for all seasons.

Everybody is not going to be a Parks, or a Hansen, or a Van Der Zee. Certainly, not Bert Andrews. That's not my objective. My work, by and large, does not pretend to be an art form. With some exceptions, they were done for the narrow purpose of creating reasonable publicity visuals for the print media. Within the parameters of that purpose, certain rules were involved. The photos should be light, and not too dark for the backgrounds. If possible, there should always be a woman in the picture, simply because the newspapers prefer it that way. Three men in a photo simply doesn't work for the print media.

These are functional, journeyman pictures from a hard-working photographer who had to overcome many technical obstacles and occupational hazards to shoot them. Some time ago, I used to take some awful chances to get a good picture. In 1970 when I was shooting *The Me Nobody Knows* in a small Village theatre, I was gaping down into my twin lens reflex camera and backed right off the stage into the orchestra pit. I was laid up for several months with a broken shoulder. During that period, I had fallen off so many ladders or walked into doors, that I went into analysis, where I discovered I was going through episodes of self-destruction. I quickly got out of that groove. But my work ethic persisted. And my enthusiasm for making journeyman photos prevailed. These photos may not all exist as art, but their principal value is that they exist at all. These photos are now part of a historical record of the development and continued growth of the Black Theatre. Many of them *are* great pictures and, if I may say so myself, have merit as art, though their original intention was simply as functional publicity photos.

I have a great photo of James Earl Jones in *Paul Robeson*. On this occasion, I had a chance to see the show beforehand and pick my shots, a luxury I don't very often get. Right after the show Jimmy was sitting wearily on a chair at the edge of the stage. He was waiting to get started with the shoot. I walked over and began chatting about the play, and reminded Jimmy of a moment in the play when he had tears in his eyes that I wished I could have captured during the performance. Since it was a one-man show, I wasn't allowed to shoot during the performance because the shutter noise would be too intrusive and distracting. Jimmy weighed my enthusiasm for the scene and said that if I really liked the tears, I should go away and come back. I slowly walked to the back of the theater, turned around, and came back down front. Jimmy was just sitting there, gripping that chair with all of his might and the tears were rolling down his face. That's how I got that terrific picture. I remain fascinated with how some actors can cry on demand.

The loss of my work in the fire was quite painful. Not only was the work valuable as history, but it also had something to do with self-definition, a way to chart my own development between the fifties and eighties. It's interesting how you begin to miss certain photos that you didn't miss until you have a need for them. So many of the early photos in Harlem will never be recovered, like Noble Sissle, Eubie Blake and Sugar Ray Robinson doing a little dance, kicking up their heels at a Harlem party. One of the classic photos was taken down the street from the Apollo Theatre at Showman's, where several major black comedians had come together for a Willie Bryant party. The great George Wiltshire, who was married to the actress Ernestine McClendon, who became the first black talent agent in New York during the fifties, had hired me to shoot the picture. Along with George, the shot included other great comics like Pigmeat, Butter Beans and Suzy, Dusty Fletcher, and Willie Bryant himself down center. When I realized that such moments would never be recovered, Harry Brown's book, *How I Found Freedom In An Un-free World* came to mind. Brown's basic thesis suggests that if you need something from a particular society, then you need to learn the rules of that society and go after what you want. And to know what you want, you've got to define your own worth. If my work was going to be viewed as more than window dressing, I would have to take it more seriously. Thus, I decided to try to recover as much of what was lost as possible and open the works up for public exhibition. I felt it was time to reveal to the public, and to myself, the legitimacy of thirty years of Black Theatre documentation.

Many people cooperated. First of all, immediately following the fire, Diane Aubry—a former administrator at NEC—and Terrie Williams—the former head of Public Relations for *Essence* magazine—formed "The Friends of Bert Andrews Committee," which threw a party at the large discotheque Visage on a cold, wintery, Sunday afternoon. They raised twelve-thousand dollars, which helped me buy new equipment, pay bills, and generally get back into business. Fortunately, I had photos distributed to publishers for a potential book, and a few exhibitions in place, which salvaged a portion of my theatre work. Thus, I was able to acquire photos that were in the files of the Frank Silvera Writer's

Workshop, along with those from Woodie King, Jr.'s traveling exhibition through the aegis of the National Black Touring Company, a collection of photos exhibited by Hazel Bryant at the Richard Allen Cultural Center, and, of course, the extensive files of the Negro Ensemble Company. The process of recovering the photos has been painstaking because so much had to be recopied from existing prints and contact sheets in order to make new negatives. It is a difficult process—where contact sheets are concerned, almost impossible. Contact sheets are simply used to give the client an opportunity to select a particular photo from many random shots. Often, they are not sharply printed, which is not necessarily important if you are merely selecting a picture.

But copying to create negatives is a whole new ball game. I now find myself dealing with two problems at once: isolating the photos that might work technically, and identifying those that make sense historically. The process is not only time consuming, it is quite expensive. In order to support the project, I had to once again pursue grants. This time, I solicited the skills of a professional fundraiser, Joan Sandler, a long-time friend whose career as an arts administrator is widely esteemed—and correctly so, since Joan, one of the great ladies of the New York art scene, had played an enormously resourceful role in the institutionalization of Black Theatre during the early seventies when she served as director of the New York Black Theatre Alliance. When Joan accepted a position as regional representative with the National Endowment for the Arts, Gloria Mitchell, formerly executive director of Boston's National Center of Afro-American Artists, took over the fundraising for the project.

Initially, a grant from the Schomburg Library was donated to buy supplies. That was followed by a major Leadership Grant from the Ford Foundation—which precipitated a flow of grants from organizations such as Con Edison, the Joyce Mertz-Gilmore Fund, Chase Manhattan Bank, the records division of CBS, NBC, the National Endowment for the Arts, the New York City Department of Cultural Affairs, the Nzingha Society, the Black Retail Action Group, the Phillip Morris Companies Inc., the Theatre Development Fund, the New York State Council on the Arts, the New York Foundation for the Arts, and numerous other donations from individuals. Part one of the recovered collection has already been turned over to the Schomburg Library, which sponsored a public exhibition in October 1989 to alert the public to the efforts being made to recover the lost collection. I'm now beginning part two, which will represent photos collected mostly from individuals rather than institutions.

As a photographer, I suppose, I was part of an ongoing movement in the shadow of the Great White Way. Of course, at one point, I felt bitter for a few minutes for being frozen out. But I still had my institutions—NEC, New Federal Theatre, Richard Allen Cultural Center, and the Frank Silvera Writer's Workshop—which provided me both with a living and with excitement. Black Theatre was not only culturally enlightening, but also provided me with the feeling that I was part of a vital community.

It could be said that the Black Theatre community is largely responsible for resurrecting its photographic history. The photos belonged to me, but the history belonged to the community. As part of that history I have enjoyed a remarkable intimacy with the creative insights of the community and shared in its accomplishments. My association has been with such a wide variety of theatre professionals—including actors, writers, directors, producers, and technicians—that it is hard not to identify with their successes through my photos. Therefore, I am grateful for this opportunity to shed light on the shadow of the Great White Way.

Biographical Notes

BERT ANDREWS was born in Chicago and raised in Harlem. Originally a song-writer, singer, and dancer, he began studying photography while in the Army in the early 1950s. He served an apprenticeship with Chuck Stewart, one of the best-known photographers of jazz musicians. Andrews is acknowledged as the preeminent documentary photographer of the Black Theatre as well as one of the most successful commercial photographers. His Broadway photo credits include *Bubbling Brown Sugar*, *Eubie*, *Me and Bessie*, *Ain't Supposed to Die a Natural Death*, and *Ma Rainey's Black Bottom*. He is currently the photographer for all productions of the Negro Ensemble Company and Woody King's New Federal Theatre. His photographs have appeared in almost every major national and international publication, including *Time*, *Life*, and *The New York Times*.

PAUL CARTER HARRISON, playwright/director, is a native New Yorker who has had a long association with the Negro Ensemble Company, which produced his Obie Award play, *The Great MacDaddy*. His Blues Operetta, *Anchorman*, was recently produced by the American Folk Theatre. Included among his published books are *The Drama of Nommo*, a collection of essays that focus on African retentions in Black Aesthetics, and the recently published anthology, *Totem Voices*. He is currently Writer-in-Residence at Columbia College in Chicago.